You Son *of a* Preacher

Dirt and Grime
from the Church to the Parsonage

Frank Gray

ISBN 978-1-64569-774-9 (paperback)
ISBN 978-1-64569-816-6 (hardcover)
ISBN 978-1-64569-775-6 (digital)

Christian Faith Publishing, Inc.
832 Park Avenue
Meadville, PA 16335
www.christianfaithpublishing.com

Printed in the United States of America

In the Beginning

Honestly, I didn't care much about the president being shot. The more pressing issue was the marshmallow Rice Krispy treats my mom had promised to make. And after much urging, she finally walked away from the small black-and-white television set and the news of the shooting and began to make the treats. Soon, she brought me the sticky, gooey, and sweet treat. As I took my first bite, I was certain no other food in the world was better. The year was 1963, and I was five years old.

The marshmallow memory must have been the only significant event in my early childhood years because I really don't remember anything specific after that until I was eleven years old. It's as if my life began at that age. Whatever the reason for spotty memories, my life was about to change drastically.

My father was the pastor of a thriving church in Dublin, Georgia, a small town near the center of the state. Eight of my eleven years were spent in that church, and I had never thought of the possibility of leaving. And I don't remember my father mentioning a trip to Savannah. I just remember the ride and hearing my mom and dad talk about why we were going. Their conversation was about trying out; a term used by preachers when they were asked to preach followed by an election to determine if the members wanted this preacher to become their pastor.

We arrived in Savannah on a Saturday night in June of 1970 taking the Thirty-Seventh Street exit into the city. Shortly after, we stopped at a huge church on a one-way street. The church was a yellow block, three-story building, and I was amazed at the size. My mom, dad, my two younger brothers and I went in and was greeted warmly. The people were old but friendly and seemed happy we were there. I realized later it was the board of deacons and their wives, and they were there to pray for a new pastor.

The next day was exciting. A good crowd had assembled, and there must have been hundreds of boys my age or at least, it seemed. However, seven or eight was probably more accurate. It was a lot of fun meeting new friends, and I found myself hoping my dad would win the election. And I thought we had a good shot. After all, from what I could tell, my dad was a good preacher.

I remember standing outside the church waiting for the results. Soon, someone came out and announced my dad had been elected. Congratulations were plentiful especially among my new friends. The previous pastor had older children, so I guess this was new and exciting for everyone. We were moving to Savannah.

Prior to the move, I had never thought about who I was or specifically what I was. So it had never occurred to me the difference between the two. But I was about to discover that what I was would be significantly more important than who I was. This revelation, no pun intended, occurred on the third or fourth Sunday at the new church in a boys Sunday school class.

The class didn't have girls and consisted of about seven or eight boys, eleven and twelve years old. The teacher was a middle-aged man, humble, and soft spoken. Though he tried, maintaining order was difficult as one could imagine. One Sunday, I guess we may have been more rowdy than usual, and the teacher had lost control of the class.

Then it happened. The teacher called me by name. "Franky," he said kindly but with a tone of seriousness, "I understand these other boys misbehaving, but you are the preacher's son. You should set the example for the other boys." There it was. For the very first time, I knew what I was. I was the son of a preacher. What I didn't know was this enlightenment would shape my life for the next four decades.

The parsonage was a modest three-bedroom home with one bath and a small kitchen. The living room and eating area was open but small. What I loved was that we had a screened-in porch on the side of the house. I guess the previous pastor must have had the carport closed in. The entire house was only about 1,200 square feet.

Fortunately, as the oldest, I had my own bedroom. My two younger brothers had to share a room. And, with only one bath, we were always fighting over the times to bathe. Not that we were all that concerned about bathing. But when Mama said it's time, who could go last was the point of contention. I guess we were in no hurry to get clean.

The first summer in the parsonage passed quickly but was a lot of fun. We quickly turned our small front yard into a football field. And Dad had a deacon set up a basketball goal in the backyard. Some of my fondest memories is of Dad playing the game of horse with us boys in the backyard. He would also join us in the front yard to toss around the football.

My youngest brother was a toddler, but my middle brother was about seven years old. Sadly, we didn't get along well, and it was my fault. We would be grown before I appreciated my brothers. I bullied my middle brother, and it's a miracle he doesn't hate me for it today.

I like to think I made him tough, and to some degree, he had to be. He played football with my age friends and never ever cried when he was hit. And we hit him hard. He did have a friend his age who lived across the street who also was tough enough to play with us older boys, but the difference was; he did cry. And almost every time we played.

One day, when he didn't get up after a tackle, he lay there crying as he usually did which we ignored. Then we realized something was wrong. He lay in a crippled-up position and screamed every time someone tried to help him up. Soon, someone went for his mom. She became hysterical. I guess she knew it was serious. And serious, it was. One of his legs had been broken in multiple places. I think he was in a cast from his waist down for about nine months. After that incident, we didn't ridicule him for crying again.

That summer of 1970 was my favorite summer. Every night, we stayed out 'till dark riding bikes or playing ball. I was never bored, and there was always something to do. This would be the last time I would feel like a normal kid. When the summer ended, and school began in the new city, my life would be anything but normal.

Shortly, after moving to Savannah, I went to youth camp with my dad. The camp was in the northwestern part of Georgia near Columbus in a place called Pine Mountain. It was really a cool place. The cabins were on rolling hills surrounded by huge pine trees. The tabernacle was an open-air pavilion where we had church at night.

There was a nice lake that we were able swim in. There was a long dock that was perfect for jumping into the lake. It was a heavily wooded area, but I don't ever remember worrying about snakes or anything harmful for that matter. The wonderment of being young, I suppose—no fears.

There were about eight boys or so to a cabin with one counselor. I don't remember his name, but my cabin counselor was a fun guy who let us have a great time with some discipline, of course. However, we would push the envelope when bedtime came, and he had a difficult time getting us to settle down.

I remember the bathhouse being a good walk away but mostly centered among the cabins. However, it was a spooky walk if you had to go in the middle of the night. Thinking back, it was somewhat primitive, and maybe that's what made it so fun.

Every day was an adventure because of the surroundings and schedule. But it was the night that was most eventful. The evangelist was a lady who was super entertaining with puppets and her style of ministry. However, she was also serious and had a way with kids to bring them around the altar at the end of the service.

It was at the altar at that old open-air tabernacle that I experienced the complete reality of a relationship with Jesus. During that first week, I accepted the Lord "officially" and his spirit filled my soul. Only eleven years old, I knew something was real about what I was feeling. More than fifty years later, through many trials, I still feel the reality. In fact, it's more real today than ever. But there was a journey to which I was about to embark that had I known, probably would have quit at the start.

Junior High and High School Years

When I first entered the seventh grade at a new school in a new city, I was excited for the change. While I didn't know what to expect, I wasn't fearing the unknown. And it was okay at first. But soon after the school year began, I found myself defending what I was. I have no idea how the subject of my dad's occupation would surface or why it seemed to be of interest to anyone. But it was. And no one viewed this favorably. On occasion, a student would even inform the teacher a preacher's son was in the class.

In addition to being a preacher's kid, the 1970–1971 school year was challenging with integration still a new concept. However, I wasn't expecting what I experienced. There was so much hate in the school. I remember wondering how someone could hate someone else just because of skin color without even knowing the person.

Rioting was a common occurrence. The green-colored plastic lunch plates were often used as flying weapons when the fights would break out. The school year was interrupted many times as high school students would march from their campus to ours. I don't remember how many times school was dismissed early, but it was a lot.

I was a small scrawny kid and had no interest in getting involved in the fighting. My plan was to run. I figured I wasn't big enough to fight, but I was fast enough to get away. Times were bad, and I don't think my parents ever knew how bad. I wonder what they would have thought if they had seen the plates being thrown hitting students in the head and see the blood flowing.

But the real fight for me wasn't with another race. I had no problem with someone of another color unless they were a bad person, and then they could be any color. My fight was being a preacher's son. I was teased from the very beginning. It's funny how times change. In later years, being a preacher's son in school wasn't such a target of ridicule. Being a Christian even became more socially accepted.

But in the early '70s, preacher's kids were assumed to be narks—someone quick to tell a higher authority of misbehaving. I didn't care what others would do, but I could not convince anyone. I was labeled a nark whether I was or not.

It's very easy for adults to say to ignore all the teasing and be who you are. But it is never easy for a kid to ignore being ridiculed. The worst advice a parent can give is this empty persuasion where substance is missing. True, a kid doesn't need to be ashamed of who they are, but no kid can practice total oblivion.

Kids need to have a defense mechanism that will prevent damage. The damage is real whether parents believe it or not. Parents can prevent emotional damage by reinforcing self-esteem. Just toughing it out won't work. The scars remain for most if not all of life.

I know there are those who read this and believe this to be a soft approach. This couldn't be further from the truth. It's a hard approach which requires extensive effort from the parents. It requires time, listening, and understanding. Who ever thought the old cliché "sticks and stones may break my bones, but words may never hurt" made any rational sense at all?

In fact, the opposite is true. Sticks and stones may bruise and cut, but these wounds heal. Words, on the other hand, can inflict life-long wounds that never heal. I've heard everything from just walk away to just smile when you're being ridiculed. This may work for a mature adult who has developed a coping mechanism and is intellectual enough to put things into perspective. But immature kids can't do that and should not be expected to do so.

But here's the clincher; if I had simply faced ridicule at school alone, I would have been okay. If I could have felt a sense of self-worth at my church, I believe it would have offset a need to be a part of the school crowd. But it wasn't so. I was more beaten down at church than I would ever be at school.

For example, I've never once heard a church member say, "The preacher's kid is doing the best he or she can." Rather, they say things like, "That preacher's kid is bad and needs to be whipped." Or, "I can't believe they behave that way." Or, "Better yet you ought to be ashamed acting that way as a preacher's kid." As a preacher's kid, I assume that their kids must have been perfect or either they were so bad. The parents were desperately looking for a role mode and who better than the preacher's kid? I'll address this later.

I had no hope of escaping the cruelty at church. So what does the preacher's kid do? In most cases, they rebel. Just like a cornered animal, when there is no way out, they fight. The irony is this rebellion seems to validate the views of the members. They even seem to relish in this outcome. Preacher's kids are the worst—no wonder.

The teen years were tough mainly because church members were notorious for reporting the activities of the preacher's kids to their father. Some incidents required me receiving a whipping from my father. He felt he had to react to prove he would handle this in real time.

On one occasion, a deacon had gone to my father after church and told him I had called someone an ugly name. In the vestibule, my father grabbed me by the arm and gave me several licks with his hand on my backside while saying the words, "We don't talk like that."

I knew that, and I hadn't. I wasn't guilty (that time), but it wasn't the whipping that hurt. It was the look of pleasure in the eyes of the deacon as I was whipped. This whipping must have validated his role of deacon, and he was pleased. I was bitter and resented most deacons after that.

But that was only one of many times a deacon performed his self-appointed job as the guardian of the preacher's son (me). But one time, it backfired on the deacon, but he never knew it. I'm sure he thought that this news he brought to my father would certainly merit another whipping. But what he never knew was my father's shocking but funny reaction.

Our church was a three-story square building. The third floor was the social hall and Sunday school area. And on Sunday nights, it was dark up there with nothing going on. As I saw it, it was an ideal place to carry a girl for a kiss if you were too young to date. Or at least, that's how I rationalized it.

I was about thirteen or fourteen years old, and the temptation was just too great. I convinced my girlfriend to walk upstairs with me while everyone fellowshipped below after the service. We would only be a minute; I explained. And furthermore, no one would even miss us for a quick moment.

A deacon must have overheard and followed us upstairs. As soon as we kissed, he appeared and asked what we were doing. Now, I suppose deacons must be too mean to kiss or be kissed since he had no idea what we were doing as obvious as it was.

We immediately started down the stairs with him in tow. Of course, he said he would have to tell my father. I thought the kiss was good, but I wasn't sure if it was worth what was coming to me.

When it was time to leave, we all got into the car, my parents in the front, and my two brothers and me in the back. My mother mentioned that we needed to stop at K-Mart for some things before going home. On the way there, my father never mentioned a word about what I was sure the deacon had told him.

I was scared to death. But the silence was worse than the upcoming whipping. As we walked around the K-mart store, he still wasn't saying anything. That was until we were standing in line waiting to check out.

I was standing directly behind Dad. Discreetly, he turned around and said something I will never forget. "Son, if you have to kiss girls, don't do it at church." Then he turned around. And to this day, we have never discussed that moment. I believe Dad understood for once that I was a normal teenage boy. That night, he cut me some slack. That time the deacon lost, and I won; thanks to some understanding from my Dad.

On another occasion, I had a girlfriend who invited me to go with her family to a night of revival at another local church. We were seated listening to the choir sing. I reached my hand over to hold hers as I whispered, "I love this song." A few minutes later, I felt a sharp pain in my right shoulder as a man's finger poked me hard.

Shocked, I looked up to see him gesturing for me to come with him. Hesitantly, I followed him out of the sanctuary and in to a small room adjacent to the foyer. There were two other men waiting for us. They were not smiling, and I sensed something was bad wrong. I learned later; all three were deacons at that church.

Gruffly, the man asked me, "Ain't you the pastor's son from First Assembly?"

"Yes, sir," I replied.

"Then you should know better, shouldn't you?" he belted.

Know better? I had no clue what he was referring to. Before I could answer, another of the executioners asked me a ridiculous question.

"Is that your wife you're sitting with?"

Are you kidding, I thought? I wasn't even old enough to drive. But it was a rhetorical question; he knew the answer, he was just trying to make a point.

"No, I'm not married," I replied. "What did I do?"

The third man answered this time. "You were touching her inappropriately."

"What?" I railed.

"Now, go back in the sanctuary and act right like you should," the first deacon said.

I did not go back in the sanctuary. Instead, I went and stood by the car. I wasn't about to go back in.

By the mercy of God, I was not turned away from church. But I wonder how many other times this had turned others away. Why would a teenager have any desire to belong to an organization or church with these leaders? Where was the love? These deacons were more concerned about exerting their authority than potentially damaging someone's soul.

I was learning at a very young age what deacons were all about. Conversely, what I was learning did not match how their roles were described in scriptures. Maybe, they were never taught how a deacon should act and what his role in the church was. In retrospect, due to the importance of the role and the consequential damage that can result from their misunderstanding their role, a course should be taught for any perspective deacon. This was never done in any church I've ever attended, but hopefully, somewhere, they are taught.

Paul identifies nine qualifications for deacons in 1 Timothy 3:8–12. Deacons are to be dignified and manage their homes and children well, to mention a few. I have never met a deacon who met all nine qualifications or even one who met half of these. But I have met deacons who added to the list. Maybe, because they knew they couldn't meet some of the nine or because the qualifications needed to be expanded, I assumed.

On many occasions, deacons have stretched their duties from managing their own children to include the pastor's children. One deacon even tried to manage the amount of time I spent praying at the altar. On many occasions, after I had knelt in prayer, this deacon would inform me that I had not spent enough time at the altar. Now, mind you, he must have stopped praying to time me. One day, I had enough.

I was prone to outbursts, and I could feel it coming. I proceeded to tell him what a hypocrite he was and how he wasn't a good example of Christ, at all. In fact, "You have a terrible spirit," I told him. And it was true. He displayed a gruff look on his face most of the time. His words were never kind. He was always rebuking people. Unfortunately, he called me "a little punk," and he left the church. Good riddance, I thought.

I soon realized; school and church were a lot alike. The only difference was Christians ridiculed me at church and non-Christians at school. Otherwise, not much difference except church was worse. The church group expected the very best behavior, and the school group tempted for the worst behavior. So at school, I lied about what I was and usually answered no when asked if my dad was a preacher. I said he was a salesman. Close enough, I thought.

I've always believed the church should be a sanctuary of love, forgiveness, acceptance, support, and restoration. The members of the church where I attended as a kid were far from any of these descriptions. They were very controlling not just of me but especially of my dad. I know he felt pressure to make sure he did nothing that appeared to be wrong even if he didn't believe it was wrong.

My father had played in his high school band, so he supported me doing the same. I had learned to play the trombone and was looking forward to wearing the fancy band uniform. But with my participation came another dose of bitterness as church members again stole from me.

The band practiced formations for the halftime show every day after school. The formations were complicated and difficult to learn. Playing and remembering the marching direction was a challenge, but I managed to get it right. Friday night would not come soon enough to present on the field what we had mastered.

Sadly, my father never saw me perform, not one single time. While I don't remember discussing it with him, I knew the reason why. He was concerned about what the church members would think of his attendance at this worldly event. I felt cheated and for no good reason other than critical hypocritical Christians.

During the game, the band sat in the bleachers on the far end of the stadium. One Friday night as the game was nearing the end, I glanced toward the end zone. Standing in the shadows alone was the figure of a man. Upon a closer observation, I recognized the man; he was my dad. He couldn't come in, so he did the best he could and stood on the outside. At that moment, I hated and resented every single church member.

To whom does a preacher's kid go when sensitive talk and support to life's questions are needed? He can't go to his pastor because his pastor is his father, and he can't go to his father because his father is his pastor. Feelings are either demonstrated in outbursts or internally processed and hidden. Both are devastating.

I formed my opinion early in life as to what the pastor's job was like. He spent a tremendous amount of time praying and preparing for sermons. But most of his sermons fell on deaf ears. He preached love and forgiveness; the members would fight and hold grudges. He preached unity; the members formed segregated groups which left him to put back together. Then he would be accused of taking sides. He preached praise and worship; the church members sat lifeless in the pews. He preached commitment and dedication; the church members attended when nothing else came up.

Who would ever want this job? Strangely enough, I did. I can't give a specific time that I received a call to the ministry. But as young as eleven, I began to think about it.

Early on, I had no difficulty with public speaking, a requirement for preachers. I would always want the biggest part in the Christmas plays every year. Mostly, I got them. The larger the crowd, the better I performed. I loved it!

I was also vocal in school. I never had a problem sharing. While other kids dreaded being in front of the class presenting, I loved it. I loved debating and had no issue strongly defending my position. Some say I missed my calling and should have been a lawyer or politician. But I knew my calling. I wanted to be a preacher.

My high school did not have a debate team. I'm sure I would have signed up if we had. However, I did have the opportunity to debate in a political science class. One topic I remember debating was the pros and cons of capital punishment. Of course, I was defending the pro position. My teacher accused me of being dogmatic. And she was correct. I was dogmatic about whatever I believed.

Another teacher signed my yearbook with this comment, "Frank, I hope the future finds you to be a more tolerant person." Thinking back on that comment, I'm struck with the reality that the same comment is being thrown around today by the liberals some forty years later. The teacher was either prophetic or ahead of her time. I believe the latter is the case. However, she would find me in my senior years as still intolerant.

The truth is my dogmatism was a direct reflection of my church. While I despised the dogmatism, I found myself guilty of the same. The dogmatism that I displayed resulted from the legalism in the church. Yet I moved forward toward what I thought was my calling. And early on, I had opportunities which I will mention later.

Throughout my high school years, maintaining friends was difficult. The other teens in the church were often jealous of me, and the teens in school thought I was a nerd (although I don't think that term was used at the time, but it means the same). For example, the first boy I met when I moved to Savannah never could get over his jealousy of who I was. We could have been lifelong friends; instead, I haven't seen or heard from him in over thirty years.

I knew when I graduated, I would attend Bible College. I looked forward to what I thought would be an escape from being the preacher's son. I was wrong.

I met my future wife when I was in the eighth grade. She was a natural blonde with long flowing blonde hair. I asked her to go steady with me, and she did; but it didn't last long. She broke up with me after a few weeks. I laugh now when I remember riding on my bike to pick up the bracelet I had given her—my first heartbreak.

I liked a lot of girls both at church and school but was usually too shy to tell them. And I was afraid to tell Dad if I liked a girl at school. He had a vision of the girl he wanted me to like. Our ideas of that girl differed greatly. I could have never dated a girl from school who didn't go to church. Of course, this was biblically correct. I knew dating a non-Christian was not good.

I began liking a very nice girl in the church when I was in the tenth grade. She was a true Christian. She was very sweet, and maybe one of the sweetest girls I've ever met. But one day, the pretty little blonde that I had known earlier walked into my church, and that was the end of my relationship with the girl I was currently liking.

It was the first week of February 1975. Our church always had a valentine banquet, and this year was no exception. I approached the beautiful blonde and asked her to be my date for the banquet. Surprisingly, she accepted. So I rushed to break up with my current girlfriend. I will always regret how I handled that and the hurt I saw in her eyes.

On the same night, the pretty blonde gave me a small school picture of her with these words written on the back, "To a guy I like a lot, but I will love you forever," I was completely and totally awe-struck. We went to the banquet together, and I knew this would be my future wife.

As soon as I could drive, we began dating. She had no idea what she was in for nor did I. We dated my junior and senior years in high school. I don't recall having a specific conversation with her concerning my calling. I think it was just understood. Nor do I remember ever sharing my struggles and everything I held inside. Maybe things would have been different had I shared. Then again, she probably would have not understood.

She was a year younger than me and therefore a year behind me in school. She knew my plans were to attend a Bible College following graduation. She researched the school and decided that's where she wanted to attend as well. To go with me the same year, she enrolled in summer school to skip from the tenth to twelfth grade. She would seek a degree in elementary education as I pursued a degree in pastoral studies.

Neither of our parents could afford to contribute to our college education, so we both worked jobs during the summer and throughout our junior and senior years to save for college. My first job was at the fast food chain, Burger King. Her first job was working at a day care. However, my senior year, I entered a work program through the school and got a job with a local engineering company to run errands and copy blueprints.

The job was specifically designed to allow a high school senior to work for one year only for saving money for college. It was a great job, and the pay was much more than anything else I could have found. The firm was large, and I stayed extremely busy.

Of course, I was asked many times in the first few weeks where I would be attending college. I was proud to say without reservation; I was going to Bible College. I was going to be a pastor; I would proudly proclaim. But I think each time I made that statement; the devil must have laughed. Just wait and see, he must have thought.

Oddly, I don't remember ever officially proposing to my girlfriend, but I must have at some point. It made sense to me. We're going to Bible College together, and later, we'll be married. She must have thought the same.

She had a terrific family with two sisters and a brother, all younger. Her dad had not accepted Christ; however, he didn't seem to oppose our dating. However, he would come to Christ before we married. But he did oppose her going with me to Bible College but later relented. Her mother was always kind, gracious, and supportive. I had a good relationship with both, and that was important to me.

In retrospect, I'm certain my wife must have seen signs of inconsistency in me. I could be very romantic and sensitive and then go into a rage at the least of things. I made excuses for my behavior. But there were reasons; I just didn't know it at the time and therefore, didn't deal with them. Such as unsettled bitterness and anger which were nestled deep in my being like anchors holding a large vessel down.

I hated the mood swings but did nothing but deny the origin. These continued through the dating period and throughout the entire marriage. At just sixteen years old, I was a mess inside. I was not capable of having a real relationship with anyone.

Preacher's kids take a lot of abuse. Most of it is internalized. I say now and many times, there is just no one that feels right for a preacher's kid to go to for help. Many just give up and go to all the wrong places such as drugs and alcohol. I've observed that many are extremist. Their search for peace carries them on a journey as far away as possible from their roots.

How does one go from the parsonage to the bar? It's not as long a trip as one would expect. In fact, the people in both places are similar. Both are looking for something to fill an empty space within. Both are seeking an escape from a cruel world. Both are deceived with both believing everything is okay and will eventually work out.

The main difference between the folks at the bar and the folks at church is hypocrisy. The bar folks aren't pretending to be something they're not. They know where they are; they know what they are doing, and they think it's fine.

On the other hand, my experience as a preacher's son is the great majority of regular church attenders are complete fakes. The world's biggest hypocrites sit on church pews Sunday after Sunday. Only a small percentage of sermons ever reach their hearts to the point of any kind of change.

Some sing, some play instruments, some teach Sunday School, some are deacons, some are choir members, and some are just pew attendants. Most are opposite of being "Christlike." I've seen them fuss and argue. I've seen them praise and shout. I've seen them ridicule and criticize. And mostly, I've heard them criticize my father.

How can anyone expect a preacher's kid to balance all they observe and put it into some sibilance of perspective? I tried. But when a deacon pushes your father against the wall, there is no balance to be found. On many occasions, my father has gone home and sat in a chair in the dark half the night because of treatment from so-called Christians.

My most impactful observation during my teen years was that a great percentage of church members listened to sermons but rarely applied the principles espoused. They got the whole hell and heaven thing and nod and say amen. But most pertinent messages went over their heads. Especially the ones regarding Christian love and forgiveness.

Emotions run high during singing and especially during revivals. And most surprisingly, church members are stirred up when an evangelist comes. Now he preaches exactly what my dad had preached. What's the difference? Frills and emotions. Evangelists have the leverage to preach anything and everything and just walk away. They're not there for illnesses, births, or funerals. They're certainly not there when grievances occur.

Evangelists can give their best. After all, they preach maybe seven times while at the church. And many of the seven sermons have been preached many times before at many different locations. A pastor doesn't have the benefit of re-preaching a sermon until it is perfected. He must provide something new every time. And that computes to about 156 different sermons per year assuming he preaches Sunday morning, Sunday evening, and again on Wednesday evening.

Honestly, I resented the way the church members responded to evangelists as if they were something special. After all, it was my dad who was there at their beckon call. It was my dad who sat many hours at the hospital with the family. It was my dad who comforted during a funeral. It was my dad who answered the phone no matter what hour they called. It was my dad who ate cold suppers because someone called and had to speak with him and on and on. Where was the evangelists?

I've seen church members slobbered all over an evangelist inviting them to meals in their homes and giving gifts. Over time, these same church members never invited my parents or gave them gifts. This is what a preacher's kid sees!

My dad had spent many hours studying and preparing sermons and praying for the right message. Did church members appreciate the effort? That would be a resounding no. This is what a preacher's kid sees.

Church members criticized my dad for being too hard and being too soft. He could never get it right. And he never visited the people he should have. He has the wrong people on the platform. He allowed the wrong people to sing and play instruments. He's not focused on the right things. He lets certain people run the church. This is what a preacher's kid sees.

As I reached out my hand to shake hands with a local pastor at a sectional youth rally, he smiled and said, "Heard you were going to Bible college."

"I am," I replied.

"For what?" he asked.

"To be a pastor," I answered.

"Well," he sighed, "a preacher's kid that wants to be a pastor. All I can say is you're either called or crazy."

Now, this is a pastor known for not using wisdom before speaking. I remember hearing he had told his congregation one Sunday morning from the pulpit that he felt more like puking than preaching. But this one time, he had made a profound statement.

Then of all things, I left for college to become a pastor!

Bible College

With both families in tow, my girlfriend and I headed to Bible College in Central Florida. Once the families left for home, we settled in each in our respective living spaces. Her in a dorm and me in the brand-new apartments for male freshmen where I would shortly meet my five new roommates. When they all had arrived, we sat around and made the usual introductions. When it was my turn, I said I was from Savannah, Georgia, and thinking, it now safe to say; I announced that I was a preacher's son—big mistake.

Immediately, I began to face the same ridicule I had back home. My roommate whom I will call "Jim" wailed, "Just my luck, are you kidding me, my roommate is a preacher's son?" And so it began. Reputations from all preacher's kids had followed me to Bible College. I've often wondered what "Jim's" experiences had been. I never asked but assumed there was a reason for his outburst when he learned what I was. Obviously, he had disdain for preacher's kids, in general.

I was hiding all my resentment and bitterness and told myself I was okay. However, at times, I couldn't fool myself. One day in a class called "Personal Evangelism," I became annoyed by one of the homework assignments. The instructions were to find someone on the street and witness to them. The task wasn't so bad, but I thought we ought to be doing that anyway, not just for a grade.

The encounter with a person had to be recorded on a 3x5 index card. The information had to include the person's name and contact information, a brief description of the conversation, and whether the person accepted Christ, or not. A percentage of the grade for the term would be based on this assignment. I don't remember the percentage, but I refused to do what I thought was making a mockery out of witnessing. I still passed the class. This just added to my loathing of hypocrisy.

I guess since all my other work and test scores were good, my professor was curious as to why I had not completed the witnessing assignment. And so he called me aside and ask me for an explanation. I explained my feelings to him, but he wasn't happy. He said he'd never heard that before, and no student had ever refused to do the assignment. I had no problem being the first.

In another class, I was given an assignment with which I had no problem. Students had to be involved in ministry of some sort in a local church. My girlfriend and I chose a small country church about thirty miles from campus. The pastor was also my English professor. He was a terrific teacher and a good preacher.

When we arrived, he immediately put us to work. I taught the junior boys Sunday school class, and my girlfriend taught the primary girls. We were both happy with our assignments and the church, but our challenge was the expense of driving there twice on Sunday.

My girlfriend had taken out a student loan but still had to work a part-time job as did I. Fortunately, we were both employed by the college cafeteria, so we could walk to the job every day. She was a server, and I was a dishwasher. But I later became a member of the chef's team, which I loved.

Our funds were tight from the beginning but became even tighter as the year wore on. So much so that during the second semester, I had to make the decision to end our work at the country church. I had a large older car that was not good on gas, and it was just costing too much. So the following Sunday would be our last.

I intended for us to attend the morning service but not return for the evening service. Buses ran from the campus to other local churches. We would have to take advantage of this transportation and find another church to attend. That was the plan!

But the plan changed. On the way back to campus, we stopped for lunch at Wendy's and discussed our situation. I watched her do her normal thing and dip her French fries into a frosty chocolate shake which she loved to do. Yuk, I thought, nasty. It didn't even look good to me. The taste couldn't be good, I thought. But she liked it, so that's all that mattered, and I didn't say anything. However, I could tell she was sad, and I knew why. I didn't want to change churches either, but the reality was I was about to be broke.

She urged me to trust God and go back to the church where we were happy and useful.

"This is not about trust," I replied. "It's common sense." She seemed to understand, and we silently finished our lunch.

I dropped her off at her dorm and drove to the parking lot in front of the apartment building where I lived. As I got out of the car, I thought the car would be sitting there until it was time to make the journey home. But I was wrong, again.

I had a miserable afternoon and could not take my usual nap. I looked at the change I had taken from my pocket and placed on my big chest; I used as a nightstand. There it was, a quarter, a dime, and a nickel—forty cents. That was all I had. No more savings, nothing in my checking—that was it. My salary from the cafeteria would go to my tuition bill.

I struggled all afternoon with the nagging feeling that I needed to return to the small country church for the evening service. I knew my gas gauge on my car was at the quarter full mark, and if I did go, it would be on empty by the time we returned to the campus. I'm not sure why, but after a while, I decided to go.

I started the car and proceeded to pick up my girlfriend. I think she was surprised since I had been so adamant about not returning. My mood was dreary, and I took it out on her. But as usual, she was sweet and encouraging. So with very little money and not much gas, we began the thirty-mile journey to church.

As the church service began, I was in no mood to worship. In my heart, I was complaining and blaming God for my despair. So like many Christians, I just went through the motions, at least, until the benediction. Then something in my heart changed, and I let go of the inward drama and began to praise him who had brought me to this place.

God's word is always so faithfully true. When one begins to worship him, his presence is real and ever so near. I began to feel better, but for no reason other than feeling his presence, I remember surrendering my thoughts and worries. God would provide, I thought. He always does. And he did.

After the service ended, a lady who looked to be in her late fifties to early sixties approached me. Although we had been attending the church for three or four months, I didn't remember ever seeing her. Then she asked me a question. "Are you a student at the Bible College?"

"Yes," I responded.

She began to explain that she had recently retired from a large grocery chain and had received a parting bonus of $800 in addition to her retirement package. She explained she wanted to help a college student and give him or her the bonus. She had brought the money to the morning service; however, there were seven or eight students attending the service.

She said she felt confused. Was she to split up the money? If not, how would she decide to whom she would give it to? She could not decide and subsequently departed without giving it to anyone.

She went to on explain that all afternoon she prayed and asked God for guidance. She was sure she was to give the money to a student. But she had no clue as to whom. Then she heard a still small voice that said, "Give it to the ones who return to the service tonight."

As she talked, my eyes welled up with tears. All I could think was what an awesome God I served and how faithful he was. I could hardly believe it. And my girlfriend and I were the only students who attended the evening service. God knew. He always knows!

I graciously thanked her through tears. But God wasn't done yet. As we begin to leave, another lady approached us and put a one-hundred-dollar bill in my hand then another and another. We left that church that night with $1,100 which as it turned out would be just enough to sustain us the remainder of the school year.

Of course, we continued to attend the small country church and gasoline was no longer an issue as God had seen to that. I never recall seeing the lady again. Maybe, she was an angel. I don't know. But I do know God provided for our needs.

With enough funds, we continued with school and traveled the three hundred or so miles home as often as we could. Prior to one of those trips home, while praying one evening, I thought I received a message to preach. It had to do with Jesus praying to his father using the title, "Abba." This was a personal title akin to the word Dad or Daddy.

Excitedly, I called and mentioned my sermon to my dad. He invited me to preach this message on a Wednesday night during one of our upcoming breaks. Well, it was a total disaster. I bombed. And I really don't know why. I had prepared, but it just didn't come out like I had prepared.

My dad also knew I bombed. His words were, "That one needs some work." Talk about complete discouragement, I was devastated. So much for being a preacher, I thought. But I later learned that sometimes you just blow it. And it happens to everyone I was told. However, I've never known my dad to blow a sermon.

In retrospect, the failure came in my attempt to be someone I wasn't. I didn't think it was enough to just be myself. I was imitating my father even to the point of leaving the pulpit area and walking in front of the congregation as he always does. I guess I was trying to impress. I've learned since that trying to impress regardless of what you are doing will result in complete failure.

From that moment, the rest of the school year was miserable. The only bright spot was somewhere along the way my girlfriend and I became engaged to be married. My relationships with my four roommates had deteriorated to the point I needed to move out. Nothing was going right.

Fortunately, I met a guy who lived in a dorm and whose roommate had dropped out of school. This had to be better, I thought. One roommate as opposed to four would be easier. To be honest, my four roommates were total slobs. They had managed to destroy a brand-new apartment in a matter of just a few months.

The bathroom was always filthy with dirty underwear on the floor. I had to kick underwear away so I could stand at the sink to brush my teeth. The carpet was stained and dirty and food was always left just sitting around until it molded. The worst thing happened just before an early morning shower.

I opened my drawer to get a pair of clean underwear, and there were none there. I had washed frequently and never waited until I ran completely out to wash. So something else was up. Being the OCD person that I was and am, I had put my initials inside my underwear—smart move. This was how I found out what happened to all my clean underwear.

I woke up my roommates to ask had anyone seen my underwear. Quite a question to wake someone to ask. Weird! But I had to ask. It worked. One of my roommates said they may have borrowed some of mine and intended to give them back. I told him to check the back tag for my initials which he did. There they were.

That was the breaking point. I was moving. Incidentally, he offered to give them back. But who wants underwear returned that had been worn? Not me. I was infuriated. The irony was that my roommates thought I was the strange one. Borrowing was what roommates did, right? I was okay with such things as deodorant, toothpaste, and class notes, but underwear is where I drew the line.

Things were much better with my new roommate. Sadly, I don't remember his name after more than forty years, and I've often wondered what became of him. But I do remember he was a good guy and very neat. The dorm was old, and we had tile floors; but I could deal with that. My roommate was constantly sweeping and mopping. I felt at home.

The dorm also had a prayer room which I frequently visited. It was great to be alone in prayer; something I never had in the apartments. But there were other downsides such as group showers. I tried to shower at times when no one else did. Otherwise, I liked the dorm much better than the apartment.

Life at college was very much routine. I would wake early, get dressed, and meet my girlfriend for breakfast. Then we would start our first classes. We had some classes together but most separate. Daily at ten o'clock, students were required to meet in the campus chapel for a church service. Afterward, we had lunch and then our afternoon classes. We would have dinner together and turn in around seven or eight. Then we'd do it all over again the next day.

Some of the chapel services were good and others not so good. I remember thinking hypocrisy wasn't limited to my local church; hypocrites attended Bible College as well. Often, I felt we were being trained to sing, praise, and worship. Our seating was segregated. Boys sat on one side and the girls on the other. I'm not sure the purpose of the segregation. But maybe the purpose was to keep the students focused on the service; it seemed juvenile to me.

I observed the same hypocrisy there that I had observed at my home church. I saw male students lift their hands and heard them clap and shout terms such as halleluiah and praise the Lord. If I hadn't known better, I would have thought these were dedicated young men. But I knew different.

The campus was not as one might expect with a welcoming spirit from all to all. Fractions and cliques existed and were obvious. When I first arrived and began working as a dish washer, the rich kids would slide their plates toward me without speaking. I guess I was a laborer at that time and not a fellow student.

One may ask what I learned while a freshman at the highly regarded Bible College. My answer may be shocking. I learned that my emotional baggage grew larger. I did not become a better man, quite the opposite. I grew more bitter. More than ever, I questioned the authenticity of my religion. However, I shared none of this with my girlfriend.

In fact, my girlfriend took the abuse from me that should have been directed at others or no one at all. I was a very jealous boyfriend who acted out often. How she put up with all my antics was a mystery. But she was a real Christian. She was sweet and forgiving and desiring of the ministry (at that time). I believed later she was turned off to the idea of ministry which was completely my fault. Who could blame her?

One day there seemed to be an air of excitement among the teachers and students concerning the arrival of a popular pastor from another state. Everywhere I turned, people were talking about the wonderful privilege we were about to experience. This great preacher was coming to speak for us at a chapel service. I had never heard of him but was told he was the pastor of one of the largest churches in our denomination, and he was one of the most revered preachers in the entire denomination. So what I thought—big deal.

But it was a big deal for the school. They rolled out the red carpet. I can still see this pastor arriving in his limousine. As he stepped out, people applauded. He was wearing a long black trench coat. To me, he looked more like a gangster than a preacher with his trench coat and his dark black wavy hair and two body guards. Now, why would a man of God need a body guard? I thought God provided protection, silly me.

It was during this time; I began a lifelong disdain for conceited rich preachers who believe they are called to a higher level. This includes television preachers which I loathe. I find no validation for this pomp and circumstance anywhere in the scriptures. Nowhere in the scriptures is congregation size or status within a denomination a criterion for ministering. Nor is it a sign of spiritual success or completeness. What I do find is this—faithfulness.

I was in no mood to hear this man preach but had no choice. I will say he was dynamic in his presentation. He preached for over an hour which is another pet peeve of mine. I believe a thirty-minute sermon preached on God's Word is more effective. But like other evangelists, he told many stories of people being saved, healed, and delivered under his ministry. Incidentally, most evangelists are guilty of this same display of self-gratification. This type of preacher is simply a professional showman.

After the service and for several weeks, I had to hear how great this man was and what a powerful sermon he had preached. The more I heard, the more sickening it became. But that's not the end of the story. Many years later, this "great" preacher was caught in an adulterous affair. He lost his church and was dismissed from the denomination. He also made it his mission to take down another well-known minister who was also full of himself and was performing similar acts. He was successful in taking him down. The news made national headlines.

I continued the process of learning and believed the professors to be legit. Most were ministers and some pastors, although some were neither. But what I did notice was the distance between the teachers and students. I remember not feeling comfortable going to them for anything even help with assignments.

I also noticed the lunch segregation. The teachers sat in an area just for them. Now, I suppose this would be the expected at a secular school. But at a Bible College, I would think where no hierarchy would be such as this where it wasn't acceptable to break bread with students.

But the teachers were not the only segregated group. I noticed many cliques on the campus. I didn't seem to fit in. Obviously, I had a complete false perception of what a place where Christians with the same desire for Christ would be like. I suppose I had created in my mind a Christian utopia. A place where everyone was equal. A place where Christ was central, and all were respected. This school was far from that.

I quickly realized there existed a "who's who," and I wasn't ever going to be comfortable at this place. At the time, I felt I was among Pharisees and Sadducees in modern times. Looking back, I gained absolutely nothing from the year I spent at this Bible College. I would later feel more comfortable at a secular school where at least the students and teachers were real.

I found myself looking forward to the end of the school year. I internalized the bitterness and tried to focus on a good thing, a summer wedding. Being engaged to my high school sweetheart and my first real love was exhilarating. We began to discuss dates and decided on August fifth. The wedding and planning were on.

Part of the planning was our return to college as a married couple. The college had an apartment building on campus for married couples, so we applied for occupancy. I made a half-hearted effort to set up my sophomore year schedule and look for a better job off campus. I had no doubt I wanted to marry my girlfriend but had serious doubts about returning to the Bible College. But I told no one.

Finally, the school year ended, and it was time to return home. I pulled away from the campus and headed north on the interstate toward home. Tired from the end of the first year and worn from studying and completing the finals, my fiancé and I were quiet for the first hundred or so miles only speaking occasionally. What she didn't know was the declaration I had made miles back just as I pulled away from the school. I'm not coming back! I later successfully completed two degrees. A bachelor of science in business management and an associate in general studies. But it would never be the same.

The Wrong Direction

After returning home, I secured a job at a paper factory, but it was a temporary summer job. Even though I had decided not to return to Bible College, my fiancé didn't accept it and continued planning for an August wedding. On many occasions, I tried to explain to her why I wasn't returning, but oddly, I didn't know the reason myself.

There was tension between us, and we broke up several times during the summer; however, the break-ups were short and only lasted a day or so. No one else was aware. My inner struggle was more than I could handle which was causing the tension in the first place.

I knew I loved this special girl, but something was very wrong. Was it the timing? Partly. If I had a do-over, I would still marry her, but I would have waited. We were just teenagers and had so much growing up to do. More than forty years later, I realized it was my calling that was the issue more than timing. I wish I had known it then.

I was as conflicted as one can be. I wanted to be a pastor; I didn't want to be a pastor. Again, no one would understand the conflict, and therefore, I bore the struggle alone. And there was my father whom I hated to disappoint. The irony was I would disappoint him many times in the future.

My dilemma was a calculated move by satanic forces, but I was oblivious. At that time in my life, I was unaware of why Satan was so intent on ensuring my failure. I certainly wasn't special. I was not particularly talented. My personality was unpredictable. I was not consistent in my relationship with Christ. I was not an eloquent speaker. I couldn't sing a note. And I was arrogant with all the answers.

But Satan didn't care about these things at all. He knows God chooses to use the weak for his glory. I was a perfectly flawed specimen. But I was the son of a preacher. That's it. And that's what he wanted. To kill a preacher's kid's potential was paramount to his mission of preventing the spread of the Gospel.

What about other preacher's kids? All I know is thousands have left the church and turned from Christ. It seems that everyone has a story about a fallen preacher's kid. I've heard stories over and over. However, I haven't spoken to any preacher's offspring for this writing. Not even my own siblings have I consulted.

And what may be surprising to many is the lack of fellowship between children of preachers. I cannot name one single preacher's kid with whom I've had any sort of relationship much less a friendship for my entire life, not one.

In the local church, the preacher's children are in a small exclusive minority. A church typically has one pastor. A church may have many children that are the same ages as the pastor's kids, but they are in a different group. While this group consists of all types, none are preacher's kids.

Preacher's kids have no one with whom to identify. Identification is important in adolescence. To feel accepted is one of the most natural desires. I can't speak for any other preacher's kid, but this is how I reacted.

I developed a strong sense of independence. I created a hard shell. I took control. I fought back even when it was unnecessary. I stood my ground. I created a strong sense of determination. I demonstrated an "I'll show you" behavior. I was confrontational. I was quick to argue. And worst of all, I was a victim. My problems were always someone else's fault.

Every attribute that I've just described became my enemy. I had learned to make up my own mind. I conferred with no one. Consequently, I convinced myself that I wasn't called to preach. And no one would convince me otherwise.

Days of that summer passed quickly, and before I knew it, our wedding day had arrived. We married on August 5, 1977 at 8:00 p.m. on a Friday night with my dad officiating the ceremony. We had a beautiful wedding with a large wedding party. The reception was elegant and just perfect.

My middle brother was my best man, and my younger brother was our ring bearer. Three other friends were my ushers; however, none were preacher's kids. I didn't realize the absence at the time, and for many years, I was not conscious of the complete absence of other preacher's kids in my life. Would it have made a difference? Of course, having no point of reference, I can't say for sure. But I can't help but believe the comradery of someone experiencing the same things as I would have made a big difference. If nothing else, I would have had someone who understood.

After we returned from our honeymoon, plans were still in place to return to Bible College. And so we were temporarily staying with my parents. However, I began to look for a job; I knew I wasn't returning to school. My rationale was I would attend a local community college and complete my degree there.

I got in my car with no direction to go. I had not looked at ads in the paper for a job. No one had mentioned to me a business that was hiring. I was just going wherever. However, I did say a quick prayer, and it went something like this. "Lord, if it's your will for me to stay and not return to school, let me find a job today."

This is a frail prayer and is not the appropriate method for praying and seeking God's will for one's life. Seeking being the key word. When a prayer such as the one I prayed is used as a foundation for decision making, the wrong one will be made every time. And my life is proof.

A frail prayer is one without substance, patience, sacrifice, and burden. All of which are components of a successful prayer. Consequently, this frail prayer has all the components for a desired outcome. In other words, one can set up a prayer to ensure one's personal preference will be the result. And that's exactly what happened to me.

I had not set aside a time in a private place to seek God's Will. The prayer was an afterthought. After all, I was driving toward a destination before I even prayed the prayer.

God is not an answering service that one can just leave a brief message and go on about their lives. Additionally, one can't make deals with God concerning his will. This is not different than going into a fast-food restaurant that normally serves hamburgers and determining it must be God's will to eat a hamburger if one is on the menu. Sounds silly? I know. But take it from someone who tried and failed with this type of prayer.

My entire life was thrown off course by this frail prayer. The very first place I stopped to apply for a job; I was hired. I walked into the front lobby of a local dairy plant. The lady at the reception desk looked up and smiled and asked if she could help me. I asked if they were hiring and if so, could I complete an application.

To my surprise, she sent me immediately back to the superintendent's office. The superintendent hired me on the spot and asked me if I could start the next day. I told him yes and left excitedly to tell my wife. God had answered my prayer, I thought. This had to be his will. How else could this have happened?

It was almost time to pick up my wife from her temporary job. So I hurriedly headed to get her.

"Guess what?" I exclaimed as my wife got in the car.

"What?" she asked. I proudly announced my new job, and that I would be starting the next day. I went on to tell her how God had opened the door, and that he proved through this that he wanted us to stay and not go back to Bible College.

Her reaction was normal but not what I wanted to hear. Of course, she was disappointed and wanted to return to Florida. She wondered why I had not consulted with her before deciding. I didn't think it was necessary; I was the boss.

For the first of many times, I proclaimed that I was "the man of the house" and therefore, made the decisions for the both of us. I couldn't have been more wrong. Not only was I not the man of the house, I was a very immature boy with an ultra-ego with no real understanding of my role as a husband. And so went the marriage.

I took full control of "our" futures. We quickly found an apartment and moved in with piecemeal furniture. We hardly had enough to fill the two-bedroom apartment, and everything was old;

but everything seemed to be falling into place. And this was just the beginning. My taking control became a pattern.

At first, all was well. I was convinced I had made the right decision. What I did not take into consideration was from where the decision had come. Often, when things are going well, we believe God is guiding the scenarios, and therefore, we are in his will. But this is not necessarily the truth.

Satan had taken complete control of my decisions of which I was attributing to God. And his plan was working magnificently. In retrospect, I see it was Satan that ensured that I would just walk into the perfect job. It was Satan that had the perfect apartment waiting for us. It was Satan that ensured my wife would also be employed very quickly. And most importantly, it was Satan who had provided the means to prevent us from returning to Bible College.

Much like Jonah in the Bible, I was in trouble. Just like him, I chose the proverbial Tarsus over Nineveh. But different than Jonah, I continued in the wrong direction guided by sequential events of deception. I had not abandoned the idea of ministry but had rationalized my new direction as the one God had orchestrated. Time would prove me wrong, repeatedly.

Unaware, I was steadfastly marching into a storm with no protection from the strong winds and fierce rain. The sound of thunder warning me of the impending storm would crash around me, but I could not hear it. Lightening would strike and strike often, but I could not feel it. The rain would fall, and I did not notice the coming flood waters that would wash away my sandy foundation. Frequently, the wind would blow me off my course. Yet I defiantly continued in the wrong direction.

I attributed my direction to God's direction. But the true driver was my own secret rebellion. After hearing stories of many preacher's kids who turned from the church, I'm convinced it's the same for all of us. Whether we admit it or not, it's pure unadulterated rebellion. But what are we rebelling against?

While I can't answer for anyone else, I've been forced by years of failure to answer it for myself. The rebellion is against the perfect will of God. The perfect will of God for me was to become a pastor.

I know this. So why didn't it happen? Who or what prevented my journey to this destination?

It was my vision. My vision of the ministry was completely clouded by my experiences as a preacher's kid. The dirt and filth of church member hypocrisy had outweighed my desire to become a pastor, subconsciously. I would never outwardly admit this to be the culprit. Had I admitted to this would have been to give the win to the church members: they had finally done me in.

Subsequently, I created an alternative will of God that would fit my plan as it was being revealed at the time. I may not be a pastor, but I could be successful at something else. I would still serve God but in a different capacity than originally planned by God. Ironically, I never consulted God about his alternative will.

Bottom line learned, there is no such thing as God's "alternative" will. God's perfect will can never be altered, compromised, or negotiated. For much of my life, I've rationalized God's will to be compartmentalized. For example, there is the perfect will of God, the submissive will of God, and finally, the acceptable will of God. All are deceptions from Satan except for the perfect will of God.

God called me to preach his Gospel; that was and is his perfect will for my life. Funny, it's never happened, at least not yet. Seriously, it may never happen for me because of the choices I've made. But nothing or no one can ever or will ever change God's perfect will for my life.

Whether I preach or not will not change his perfect will. But because of his amazing and forgiving grace, I can function in some capacity to please him shy of his perfect will.

In some cases, his perfect will cannot be realized because of irreversible mistakes and sin. In other scenarios, his perfect will can be realized but may look different than what was originally envisioned in our minds. The encouraging fact is a preacher's kid can rebel and turn away but can also return to the perfect will of God whatever that may be.

I'm still winding my way back to God's perfect will for my life. Some may mock and laugh as years have appeared to pass me by. But I know there is hope until I take my last breath in this place where he knows who I am, what I am, and where I am. And yet he called me knowing full well all these things. How do I know? Because I've seen the *hand of God* many times in my wretched life.

The Hand of God

Kids love balloons. But balloons are temporary. And such is life. They are colorful, and when full of helium are only restrained by the ties that bind them. But when they are released soar to heights beyond the horizon, some go east; some go west; some go north; and some go south. But all are blown by the wind to unknown destinations.

Gradually, the helium leaks, and the balloons start to descend. Only the hand of God can guide the balloon of life before the final decent. This has been my life. I have felt the hand of God, and without doubt, I know his hand has always been on me. However, like a balloon, spiritually, I have drifted from place to place; lost and letting the troubled wind determine my destination.

At the age of thirteen, I had my first opportunity to teach a Sunday school class. I had a very strict but wonderful teacher. She demanded respect, and most of the kids hated her class because she would not tolerate any type of misbehavior. I respected her very much and relished at her offer to let me try my hand at teaching. As an adult, I would later have several intervals of teaching Sunday school classes.

Maybe, she thought because I was the preacher's son; this would be beginning preparation for the future. But I chose to believe she just thought I could do it. And I did. I loved it. It seemed to come so naturally. Now, as a Sunday school teacher myself, I give her all the credit for setting the example for teaching. She never rambled. She stayed with the script, and it was obvious she knew the material. She passed away a few years ago, and sadly, I had lost contact with her.

But I will never forget the influence she had on my life. She was the only church member who truly believed in me.

While my life was bizarrely inconsistent, something inside of me always led me to believe I was called. Called to what? I'm not sure even today. But the desire to minister in some way has been secretly hidden in my heart.

I've heard the expression "The Hand of God" many times. But how do you really know when this becomes reality? The best way to explain it is—you just know. And when you experience the hand of God in your life, no one can take it away or explain it away.

During mental turmoil and anguish with a splash of rebellion and resentment, one would assume the hand of God could not be seen or felt, not true. I've questioned many times why God had moved on me only to be followed by my complete and total sin and failure. The answer, God never gives up on us.

The first time I knew without a doubt God was about to use me was during a Putt-Putt game. As youth leader, I had organized a group to play Putt-Putt on a Saturday night. I guess maybe twenty or thirty showed up. I was newly married, and my wife and I was together. I was a Sunday school teacher at the time (one of many stints off and on) and had already prepared a lesson for the next day.

My lessons were always scripturally based, but I never used the curriculum provided by the church. I wrote my own and tried to have a gimmick that would create interest and be entertaining. All the while laying down a scriptural truth. And it was both effective and controversial. As usual, I was criticized. Some of the other Sunday school teachers resented me not using the approved curriculum. And I heard about it.

My technique must have been working. My class was growing. I started with a class of about eight or so but soon after reached twenty then thirty. Suddenly, I realized we could reach for a goal of fifty. I announced the goal and had buy in. I even said we would have a '50s party to celebrate when we reached the goal. Of course, that too was controversial. And again, I heard about it.

We started a visitation program, the old-fashioned kind. We went door to door to invite young couples to come and join us. I was riding high. And soon on a Sunday morning, the fiftieth person walked in. And we did it. We celebrated with a '50s party. The girls wore the poodle skirts, and the guys slicked back their hair. We even played a '50s game. How many people could be stuffed in a telephone booth? Again, per the decade. Of course, we didn't have a phone booth, but a closet worked just fine. Now, how they did it? I don't have a clue, but twenty-seven people forced themselves in a closet two-by-four-by-eight feet tall. We took pictures. It was hilarious and a whole lot of fun.

It was shortly after this huge success that I was playing Putt-Putt. Strangely, I had a strong urge to go home and change my lesson plan. I fought the urge, but it wouldn't go away. Finally, I mentioned it to my wife and told her I had to go home. We were still playing, and I'm sure she wanted to stay. But she sweetly relented, and we went home. Although, clearly, she didn't understand what was happening.

We had a modest three-bedroom one-bath house, and I went into the small bathroom to pray and ask God what this was about. I never heard an audible voice and still haven't at the time of this writing. But the feeling was so strong. I didn't need a voice; I could sense something was happening.

I found a pencil and scratch paper and begin to write what I was feeling. I was led to Acts 2:4. I knew I needed to change my lesson to address being filled with the Holy Spirit of God. I could hardly write through tears. There is no feeling in the world equal to the feeling of the touch of God's hand.

The next morning, I awoke with the same overwhelming feeling. But I began to doubt if this was real or just some emotional high. I had been prone to emotional swings. How would I know?

I arrived early for Sunday school but did not want to do my usual thing. Normally, I would welcome each one as they arrived. I would joke and usually have a gimmick handout to give as they entered the room. For example, I would give each one a piece of peppermint candy while trying to extrapolate a farfetched connection to the scriptures from the colors and taste of the candy. I later realized gimmicks work but don't last.

But this Sunday, I found someone to pray with me to make sure I was about to do the right thing. I found a man, another Sunday school teacher and asked him to pray with me. The irony is, while he didn't say, this man had lost faith in me and rightly so. He knew my track record which was inconsistent at best even though recently I was on track. I'm sure he must have thought this was another grandstand. But he prayed with me despite that.

I waited for all the attendees to arrive before entering the room. I walked up to the podium and said, "Today is going to be different. I feel led to do this. I will skip the formalities and go straight to the scripture God has laid on my heart." They were stunned, and I was petrified. But I proceeded.

For the next twenty or so minutes, I taught on the importance of being Spirit-filled. Then I asked them to bow their head while I prayed. "Lord, I know you have spoken to me with this message that I have delivered today. Now, let each one here experience what I have spoken of." Nothing happened.

I began sweating nervously. Apparently, I was on my own and was making a fool of myself. So I tried something different. I asked each one to kneel at their seat and pray. They responded. Still nothing happened.

Not only was I becoming desperate, I had no clue where to go next. Then a strange phenomenon occurred. People began weeping and praying aloud—confirmation. I had heard from God. And his *hand* was touching this class.

The time of prayer continued and lasted until long after the service in the sanctuary had ended. It was fantastic! I was seeing the reality of following the urging of the Spirit of God. But it was short lived and shortly after, I began to fail again. This began a series of being used of God followed by failure.

My wife was a Sunday school teacher for the young children and was not in the room when this happened. I've often wondered if her presence would have made a difference or would I still have failed. I was really confused.

For every victory, Satan found a way to detour me, and this was no exception. One of the members of my class innocently began to compliment my teaching. It felt good. She would tell me how she wished her husband was more like me. I relished in the compliments. I thought my own wife didn't do this. But how could she? She wasn't in my class. This is called rationalization also known as justifying.

Innocence is relative. And when Satan is involved, what starts out innocent ends in anything but. To be more specific about this account would serve no purpose. To describe details would make me worse than those hypocrites of which I write in this book. I intend to be transparent when I say I failed but refuse to give Satan the glory by revealing details. If that's what you're looking for, you're reading the wrong book, and you'll be disappointed. My intention is to uplift, not tear down.

Suffice it to say, I failed. I take full responsibility and blame only Satan and my own weakness. I wish I had learned long ago that people including church members were not my enemies; it was Satan all along. Of course, he used many along the way, but he is the genesis of all wrong and temptations.

Some years later while still a young adult, I felt the hand of God again. A lady in the church had given me a picture on a wooden frame. It was nice and appropriate for a dining room, so that's where I hung it.

The picture was that of a long elegantly set dinner table. The table seemed to go forever in the distance and appeared to have no end. The table was set formally as if special guests were to arrive for dinner. The dinner plates looked like the finest china had been selected. The tablecloth was gold with glittered stitching. The cloth napkins matched and were wrapped in what appeared to be pure gold holders. Candleholders adorned the table as center pieces. These too were gold with gold candles. The candles were lit as if the guests would be arriving soon.

One night, I got out of bed and went into the kitchen for a glass of milk. I poured the milk and set at the kitchen table to drink. As I took my first sip, I glanced up at the picture I had hung several weeks before. To this point, it had been just a pretty picture. But this night, I saw something completely different. It was not a picture of just any table, it was a picture of the Marriage Supper of the Lamb in the Bible. Or, at least, that's what it was to me.

As I gazed, I begin reflecting on what I had heard and been taught about this supper prepared for the Bride of Christ. Then I thought of all the surrounding events relating to this event. I thought of the second coming of Christ, the Judgement Seat of Christ, the Great White Throne of Judgment, And I thought of the final destinations for all men, heaven or hell.

It occurred to me that a dramatic presentation would be just the thing to depict these prophetic scenes. And so I began to write creating characters, scenes, props, and sound effects. The result was a play which I called *The Journey.*

At the time, we had a good size youth group so why not perform a play. No experience needed. Not that we had any experience anyway, especially not me as a director. But I pressed on with my idea, and surprisingly, everybody seemed excited.

Later in life, I was posed this question, "Are leaders born or trained?"

I answered quickly, "Leaders are born. You cannot train leadership instinct," I said. I guess I based this on my own experience because I had never had formal leadership training, but I not only led but loved it and was successful. People seemed to naturally follow my lead and *The Journey* was my first true indicator.

The Journey consisted of seven scenes. A church choir scene, a home scene, a mark of the beast scene, a Great White Throne judgment scene, a Judgment Seat of Christ scene, a lake of fire scene, and the finale, a pit of hell scene. My imagination went wild as I wrote each line of every scene, and I was determined to bring it to life.

We first performed *The Journey* in 1979 with reproductions in 1980, 1981, and one final time in 1996 under a slightly different title, *No Escape from Hell.* With each performance, the acting, sets, props, and sound effects all improved. The first production was juvenile; we just threw together costumes, make-up, and cardboard painted fire. The flames on the cardboard were painted in a church member's garage approximately seven or eight blocks from the church by the cast (no painters).

Without any thought of transport to the church, we just painted the taped-together cardboard. Upon completion, the only option was to walk the monstrosity to the church. This walk occurred at three o'clock in the morning. And it was cold. But our spirits were determined, and we made the successful tract. This is one of my fondest memories.

Thinking back, it was one of the most exciting times of my life. As juvenile as it was, it was mine; my idea from God coming to life, and I was thrilled. I was so young at the time, just twenty years old, but I knew I was being led by God; his mighty hand was on this very simple endeavor.

The first big challenge was to create a lake of fire for which to throw people in as the Bible describes. Well, I thought the baptismal pool was the perfect place. But how? Kool-Aid, of course. Many bags of cherry flavored Kool-Aid. In retrospect, it was the dumbest idea I had (among many), but it worked. At least, the water was turned to red. But how would we make it look hot? That was easy, I thought. Just obtain an air compressor and attach a hose to it to blow into the water.

Fortunately for me, I had a best friend who was a plumber. Somehow, he would take my ridiculous sounding ideas and make them work. And the lake of fire was no exception. He secured a 2x12 board that would reach across the top steps of the pool. He laid the board just beneath the top of the water. Genius! This gave the appearance the characters were walking across the water and just dropped in.

He secured the hose to the bottom of the pool and thus a bubbling pool of red water. However, the characters looked hilarious after taking a plunge. The sugar Kool-Aid turned them all red, not exactly the intended outcome. We learned later to use a different method for coloring the water. But I must say the participants were always willing even when the heater malfunctioned during a performance.

I must skip to the overheating before going on. During one of the performances, the thermostat stuck, and the water reached 120 degrees. It was hot, and as the narrator, I was watching from the front pew thinking these people were giving their best performance of suffering yet. Better than I'd seen in any practice.

Well, they were not acting; they were really getting burned. Fortunately, no one was injured, but it made for a tremendous effect. After all, as a director, that was all I cared about. However, I certainly didn't want anyone hurt. But I was accused of the heat; everyone knew I wanted it realistic. But I really didn't do it. I did think about it later but was advised against it.

The hot pool was just one of many funny things that happened along the way, but the results from the attendees was something no one expected which I will describe later.

How do you make people disappear? We had to answer that question if we were to ever pull off the "rapture." We started with the idea that a youth choir would be singing, and suddenly, half of them would disappear leaving the others left behind and terrified. I'm not exactly sure who came up with the idea to use the lights, but here's how it worked.

At a precise moment in the song, a stage person would turn off the lights on the stage. At that moment, the entire building was totally black. He would count four seconds and turn lights back on. It worked.

When the lights went off, half of the choir ducked down behind the pews, and the bannister blocked them from view from the audience. The choir director, who was my middle brother, ducked into the pulpit. To this day, it's a miracle that he could fit into the tiny space, but he did every time flawlessly.

The intended result was a success. It really gave the illusion that people had suddenly vanished. From the vanishing or rapture to the finale with people moaning of regrets in hell, the audience was captivated. More importantly, they were touched.

When the very first performance ended, my father and our pastor gave an invitation for those who had not accepted Christ to come. And come, they did by the droves. The first crowd numbered around four hundred but steadily grew to twice the number before we ended.

We started with the idea to perform the play on a Sunday night, a onetime event. But God had other plans. And we began a three-day showing including Saturday, Sunday, and Monday. The response was overwhelming. It became a revival rather than a play. At one point, we had to ask our church members not to attend to give others a seat.

God's hand was evident taking this simple little play with simple props and no real actors and turning into a soul-reaching revival. We don't know the number of people who accepted Christ during these three years, but we know there were many.

More than thirty years have passed since the dramatic presentation of prophetic events. However, we occasionally still meet those whose lives were changed because of the production. One such meeting occurred in the mid-eighties to me while I was a meter reader with a local utility company.

As I was reading and walking on a downtown street, I saw and heard a man standing on a street corner attempting to tell people about Christ. Considering him to be a radical or nut and seeking to avoid confrontation, I tried walking behind the houses so he would not see me. But see me, he did. I couldn't escape.

When he saw me, he shouted out, "Hey, I know you." I thought, just my luck; this nut thinks he knows me. I was polite and shook his hand. "You're the guy who did the play on hell and heaven at First Assembly, right?"

"That's me," I replied.

"Man, that was great," he said. "I accepted Christ one night after seeing the play, and now I'm telling others about Jesus." I was completely blown away. At that time, more than six years had passed since the last production. And here stood a guy witnessing all that time later after being saved at the play.

To me, that one experience was complete validation that the hand of God was upon me and the play. But there were many stories of validation that exists to this day. Even my dad refers to that time frame as one of the greatest in our church's history.

I've had questions concerning the hand of God many times throughout my life. I've never questioned his divine intervention or the reality, but I did question the inconsistency of his hand touching my life. I would question why God would move me to do things such as write a dynamic play or to teach a powerful Sunday school lesson only to be completely non-existent in my life at most other times.

But it wasn't the inconsistency of God; it was my inconsistency that prevented his hand to touch my life. God cannot move upon that which is not holy. And many times, my life and my thoughts were not holy. God cannot move upon a heart that is rebellious and resentful and full of bitterness. My heart was often consumed with all of these.

To understand how the hand of God touches, the condition at the time of the touch must be analyzed. In my life, he touched me and used me to perform things outside of my abilities when my heart was open and ready. For example, when I was moved upon to write the script for the play that brought revival to our church, my marriage was right (at the time). I was treating my wife as I should. But that didn't last and neither did God's touch.

Unfortunately, when God uses a preacher's kid and then the preacher's kid fails, the failure is amplified throughout the church. I have no doubt that I am just one of hundreds of thousands of preacher's kids who at some point was used by God. But later turned away from serving him in the capacity God desired. The pressure to succeed was too much.

But to all who have failed and never returned, the touch of the hand of God cannot be denied. The hand of God was premeditated and therefore, will still touch when the wayward comes home. Here is the central point. God never touches and leaves.

Some preacher's kids have felt the call for pulpit ministry and felt his mighty hand of anointing as I did but later strayed far from the call. Others had beautiful singing voices and once sang for the glory of God. Still others were tremendous musicians who were mightily used by God but turned to make the millions from the secular world. So many preacher's kids, so many talents, so many lost. But why?

They chose to go down a path where the hand of God could not follow and bless. However, these same wayward preacher's kids are still chosen, and the hand of God can still touch them if they will just return to a place where he can. They have not gone so far as they cannot return to him.

Of course, God's touch is for anyone, but I obviously have a special place in my heart for preacher's kids who have left the fold.

However, God's touch is also for those preacher's kids who have not left the fold but are holding on to grudges, bitterness, and disappointments.

This group for me is almost just as sad as the wayward group. They live their lives under the cloud of dissolution and deep pain. They cannot let go of their childhood experiences in the parsonage. They have validated their lives even successfully but have a secret hole in the middle of their hearts that they believe no one understands.

I can identify with this group. I've never completely left the church, but I've carried much baggage for many years. Only a few years ago have I been completely delivered from the past. Before my deliverance, I was miserable. First, because I believed I missed or lost the calling. Second, I believed there was no hope for me to return to the calling. But I was wrong on both accounts. I'll elaborate later.

To receive deliverance, I had to be willing to face the past for what it was—failures. I had to accept the blame and to do so meant to painfully revisit the experiences where I was both right and wrong. To live in the light, I needed to revisit the dark and understand what happened and why.

The Youth Pastor Disaster and the Darkest Years

Married only a year or so, my wife and I was standing around the altar on a Sunday morning during what used to be called the altar service. My dad had invited a "big name" evangelists/pastor from the state of Ohio. We had never met or had been introduced prior to this morning service.

While I was standing there, this evangelist slowly walked toward me, stopped, and stared right into my eyes. He was standing so close I could feel his breath on my face. I became uncomfortable not knowing what he was about to do or say. Then slowly and deliberately, he began to speak in a low and fearful tone. He said, "Be careful, Satan has desired to sift you like wheat."

These were not unfamiliar words to me having studied the apostle Peter. I had read in the Bible where Jesus spoke these same words to the disciple, Peter. And I had heard this text preached many times.

Now, I've never been inclined to think much of this kind of thing, words from God through another. I always thought God could tell me himself. But I was wrong, and these were words to which I should have heeded. Honestly, the preacher scared me to death, but I almost immediately dismissed his words as just drama from a demonstrative preacher who was known for strange antics during his sermons.

Once during a sermon, he lunged for a guitar on a stand and began to swing it around. This was an expensive guitar, and I think we all drew a collective breath. However, he didn't damage the guitar. And I don't have a clue what his point was but using inanimate objects was part of his charm and effectiveness, I suppose.

At any rate, despite his antics and technique, he obviously was moved upon by the Holy Spirit to speak the words to me. I know this because the words struck home for me many times over many years. But at that time, I was young and cocky and invincible in many ways in my eyes. I didn't believe I could be overcome by the devil. Little did I understand how I would be sifted like wheat just like the wild evangelist had spoken.

More than anything, the evangelists had sent me a warning. The warning was unknown by all but me. I knew what was wrong. My heart was diseased. I just wouldn't admit it.

My wife had no idea she had married a man with spiritual heart disease. A man who was torn between worlds. A man who wanted to do good but could not find escape from the scars and repetitions of successes and failures. A man often accused of running away from the call. Little did they know I was running to and from the call simultaneously most of the time. I had never tried explaining anything to her. So, in her defense, she never had the opportunity to understand or help. But I don't think she could have done either.

My mom is the one who diagnosed me with heart disease. She would say something I despised to hear. "When things are right with the Lord, everything else will be right," she would say. And I would argue my point with her. After all, she couldn't possibly understand. She couldn't understand, but she knew the cause. I only knew the symptoms. Years later, I discovered how right she had been.

After the success of *The Journey*, things were good. The youth group was active, and I was the leader. I guess it must have seemed to be a natural step for me to work full time in that role, and so it happened. It was a complete disaster in every respect. My father/pastor had now become my boss. More than ever, I was performing in a cage, and the reviews were not good. The pressure was intense.

I failed (again), and this time, I was pushed out and rightly so. Everything began to fall apart. I got my old job back at a local dairy plant, but nothing was going right for me. I was a terrible husband

and not a very good father to my infant daughter. What was wrong with me? I really didn't know. I just knew the church had failed me.

Ultimately, I was separated from my wife, and at one point was homeless. Me, a preacher's son from a good home, homeless. I couldn't go home; Dad could not be perceived as condoning my failure, and he held his ground. Any other son who failed would have been embraced by his father without condemnation. But not me, I was the son of a preacher. By proxy, the church members had decided.

Desolate, I spent the first night in my truck. I reeked of bitterness and again felt robbed by the church even though what had come upon me was nobody's fault but my own. Fortunately, the separation was short lived as my wife agreed to try again. While I was contrite and grateful for her willingness, I was still very broken.

What went wrong with my first full-time ministry job? It would be decades before I faced the hard facts or really one fact. It was my fault. It was not the church's fault meaning the members. It was not my father's fault. I brought on every stress I felt on my own. But why?

It began with my own inability to accept my immaturity. I was so responsible in so many ways. I held a job. Financially, I provided for my family. I paid my tithes, and I paid my debts. We had a nice starter home. But in every other way, I was immature. A little insecure boy in a man's body.

What I didn't know then is the criticality of the development of the whole person. The most important aspect is the spiritual development. No one can ever be whole and approach life in an adult manner until they are whole spiritually. And I was not. I had a head knowledge probably higher than most. I knew the scriptures. I was confident in my faith, but I was lacking humility.

Simply put, I had a huge ego. I thought I was right in just about everything. My innate leadership fed my decisions and caused chaos in the church. I believed if someone didn't support whatever I was trying to accomplish, they were wrong.

The challenge with innate leadership abilities is self-control. The difficulty of asking others and considering other opinions is a catalyst that drives failures at an epic level. For example, music is an interesting and necessary component of any church. Yet it can become one of the most controversial aspects of the organization.

My brother and some other talented singers had adapted a Beach Boys song to a gospel message. I thought it was terrific. They sounded terrific and sang the song acapella in perfect pitch, or least, I thought so. However, some church members were offended which resulted in a meeting.

My father was placed in the middle of the conflict as one of his sons was the youth pastor and the other a singer in the group that was offending. I was adamant that the song was okay. The ones offended were being narrow minded and ridiculous. I made matters worse by acting out loudly. I never considered the feelings of the ones offended. I just saw them as challenging my authority to plan youth services.

I remember well my brother being hurt deeply by the insinuation that something was "sinful" about what he was doing. He wept on my dad's shoulder, and I'll never get the image out of my head. I heard him say calmly and humbly, "Dad, I don't understand."

There was no understanding as far as I was concerned. Just another critical church member against us. Of course, it wasn't that at all. The church member must have genuinely believed a compromise was being made that would be hurtful to the youth of the church. I didn't believe that at all but never considered the opposing view.

This is a dream of a do-over for me that I will never have. But if I could, I would have worked toward a pleasing compromise that would have worked for all involved. I would have seen the devil's hand trying to divide us, and I would have not been a part of it. But I was. However, my failure to play the adult part instead of a whiney kid caused pain.

I believe this one incident scarred my brother for a long time if not forever. Maturity would have enabled me to see this and act proactively. I would have protected my brother's innocence, and at the same time helped the church member to see what the goal was. We were all on the same team; I could have explained.

The devil through church members exploited my immaturity. I was doomed from the beginning. From the day of the announcement of my hiring, I was sure to fail. The hiring premise was wrong. The deacon board who hired me had a set of expectations that no preacher's kid could have achieved—perfection.

As the youth pastor, I was on a pedestal. I thought deservingly so. In my heart, I believed I would succeed. Even having dreams of one day succeeding my father. But my spiritual maturity was nowhere close to that of my father's.

My prayer life was slack. My Bible reading was slack. How could I expect to counter the church members? Although I didn't see them as the enemy until later. Had I been humble and submissive, the church members may have been more supportive.

On the other hand, the church members do have a level of responsibility to support the ministry. As brutal as my failure was, theirs was equally ugly. I believe a preacher's kid is at the mercy of the church membership to a great degree. This does not eliminate or even minimize the preacher's kid's personal responsibility. But the two must work together to defeat the devil who is out to defeat the kid. Believe me, I know.

I failed in my first attempt in the ministry for many reasons all beginning with me. I offer no excuses and have no reasons that seem pliable after all these years. My spiritual life was weak causing my marriage to be weak. I can't cast blame away from me.

Understanding what went wrong and who was to blame did help me move forward. I believe this is the missing link in the lives of many preacher's kids who have turned away from the Gospel. Here is the bottom line for me. Church members hurt me. Church members many times were against me. But I could have risen above the opposition had my heart been right.

Therefore, no one should cause another to stray from what their true calling is. Oddly, this phenomenon seems to be more prevalent in the church than in the secular world. Preacher's kids are hurt and distracted and ultimately exiled either by proxy or their own volition.

But are politicians' kids? What about lawyers' kids? The list goes on. What people say in the secular world seems to have less impact to the outcome of careers as what church members say. Find a preacher's kid and ask them why they're not in the ministry and why they don't go to church. My money is on them saying something about the church, it's hierarchy, or its membership.

Throughout the short year I spent as youth pastor, I constantly fought with the members. It must have been so difficult for my dad. And it ended badly with him asking me for my resignation. In the end, I left very bitter. At the time, I thought I would never have another shot at ministry, but I would be wrong again!

Another Chance, Another Failure

Out of the blue, I received a call from a young lady from a Church of God just outside of Savannah. By now, things were relatively okay at home, but I was not involved in any type of ministry and was beyond miserable. But no one knew. Anyway, this call was just the spark I needed. I was requested to teach and produce Christian drama for a youth group. Excitedly, I agreed to do so and promised to meet with the group within a week.

It felt great. Now, twenty-six years old with my life in front of me, here I go, I thought. I met with the group, and it was all thumbs up. I recruited my best friend at the time to join me which he did. I wrote a new drama just for the group called *Two Glass Eyes.*

It was a simple play with a basic message about spiritual vision. Nothing too deep, but a message that the kids could get their arms around and one easily communicated to an audience. The main character was a young person with a literal glass eye who was ridiculed by the group. In the end, the group learned that blindness from a spiritual perspective was more devastating than a physical blindness could ever be.

I was amazed at the group, and the opportunity I was given. These were terrific kids who yearned for mentorship. And I wanted to provide exactly that to them hopefully having learned from my previous stint and failure as a youth leader. This time I had no intention of failing. I had learned a measure of humility and began to depend on God for guidance.

The challenge was to teach these teenagers between the ages of thirteen to sixteen to act. They tried hard, and once again, I believed

God's hand was on this. It worked. The presentation was a huge success, and the parents were elated. Subsequently, I was asked by the pastor to become the youth pastor.

By now, I was working as a meter reader at a local utility company and had great hours, so I buried myself into this youth ministry. I started a choir, a Bible study, and continued with a drama group. The group grew to about eighty teenagers, and they were mine to teach. Though more than thirty years ago, I still cry when I think about the lost opportunity. And I wonder where these kids are today and if they are serving the Lord.

We called the group "Royal Reflections." We had beautiful T-shirts made with a pelican, and its reflection on the front. We wore these proudly. The kids even wore them on certain days to their high school. Enthusiasm spread throughout the church. The kids were turned on to the programs, and the parents were supportive. The Royal Reflections became a powerful youth group.

I loved the pastor, and because he was not my dad, things were so much easier. We had a great relationship, and he supported all my efforts 100 percent. Not that my dad did not support me, but nepotism or the hint of it always was a barrier. I don't believe it's impossible for father and son to work together in the ministry. Some have been very successful working together. But I believe the smaller the church, the tougher it is to do.

The congregation has a difficult time separating the pastor from the son. Whatever the son speaks is a direct reflection of the father. Very unfair but real. They are almost perceived as one person. Even when tried within the family, total objectivity is virtually impossible to achieve.

I know my dad tried and so did I but to no avail. Due to my young age and immaturity, my dad was constantly stressed over what I might do or say. He knew we were linked unlike pastor and youth pastor who were not related. Our personal conversations were always tense, and my dad overcompensated for the relationship.

I remember before the first meeting with the deacons; he admonished me to remain silent unless I was spoken to. I was very resentful as I felt he was treating me like a child. More importantly, this would have never occurred if I was not his son. Moreover, if a pastor must issue that warning, the individual who is the youth pastor probably should not be in the position in the first place.

Miraculously, my dad and I survived together in the ministry for a short time. I understand now the tremendous pressure he must have felt. And I didn't make it any easier for him. Yet he had confidence in my abilities despite most of my actions. I didn't appreciate our situation until I had my first opportunity at a new church with a non-relative pastor.

Retrospectively, in the end, the failure to work with my dad in the ministry was neither his fault or mine. Neither of us knew what to expect both from each other and the congregation. Everything was trial and error and mostly error.

The new opportunity was so different than anything my father and I had experienced. Not necessarily because I had grown and matured and not because the new pastor had some superior skill set. The difference was simple. No one said, "You son of a preacher." No one cared that I was a preacher's son for once because my dad wasn't the pastor. It was exhilarating.

For the first time in my young life, I didn't feel like a preacher's kid. As I reflect on this time of freedom, sadness filled my being. No preacher's kid should ever feel the need to run away and find this freedom. I'm ashamed this happened to me, and I felt so desperate to disengage completely from what I was.

How many other preacher's kids have felt the same way? Get away from here! As far away as possible. Maybe, where no one identifies me as a preacher's kid. Like me, I'm very sure there are literally thousands who have sought for self-independence away from the church.

At the new church, I felt completely liberated. But it wouldn't last. No one can run far enough away without embracing who or what they are and expect the past to never catch up with them. The scenarios change, faces change, but the root issue remains. I will be a preacher's kid until I die, and nothing will ever change that. It's what I do with it that will make or break me. I had to face it head on. But

I wasn't ready, and things were really beginning to be good for me. I was in ministry, and it was working for me.

The vibrant youth group seemed to ignite the entire congregation. Our services were great! Thinking back, it was almost heaven—just perfect. My life was fulfilled. I was complete. I had no enemies or, so I thought. I was anointed to lead, and I was thrilled. But the euphoric world I was living in would be short lived. I would crash and burn, again. I didn't see the crash coming. How could I? Everything was so perfect.

During my early childhood, I wanted to preach. I can't pinpoint the time or any significant calling. I just knew. The one bright spot during the time I worked with my dad was an opportunity to preach on a regular basis for a time. Unfortunately, my opportunity came at a great cost to my dad.

At a church social, we were enjoying a game of coed softball. My dad was just forty-one years old at the time and was very active. In fact, he was the pitcher for one of the teams. I was on the other team. Something I will regret for the rest of my life involved my competitive spirit getting the best of me.

I was running the bases headed for home when the ball was thrown back to the pitcher, my dad. As I rounded third base, I realized he had the ball. I thought I could score so I headed for home plate. At the same moment, my dad took off after me to prevent me from scoring. He was equally competitive.

Suddenly, disaster struck as our bodies collided between third base and home. My dad won and lost. He won by tagging me out. He lost when my body struck his right leg. Tragically, in a split second, his tibia and fibula bones were completely broken. We all heard a loud popping sound as his bones broke.

As I began to get up, I realized how bad it was. All my dad said was, "My leg is broken." We called 9-1-1, and the ambulance arrived shortly and carried him to the hospital.

My dad would be in several casts over the next nine months. He suffered great with the pain and bouts of depression. A very active man was for the first time in his life was completely disabled. Most of all, he would not be at church behind the pulpit doing what he loves best, preaching.

That's where my opportunity came. I visited him in the hospital later that same day, and of course, he was concerned about the next day, Sunday. Without hesitation, he looked at me and told me I would be stepping in for him. Then, he invited me to use a sermon he had already prepared.

The next day was the first Sunday of the month; the Sunday when we observed Holy Communion. Appropriately, Dad had prepared a sermon suitable for the occasion. He told me where to find the sermon. I went to his house and found it just where he said it was. The title which I will never forget was, "New Things from the Cross." I was extremely honored to preach his sermon.

I don't remember exactly how many times I preached in his place, but it was several times beginning on that Holy Communion Sunday. The validation I felt was indescribable. I knew nothing would ever make me feel the way I felt behind the sacred pulpit. And through all the ups and downs in my life, this truth remains.

At the new church, I was about to have the opportunity to preach again. The pastor approached me about preaching one Sunday night monthly. He suggested making the last Sunday night of each month youth night. I was ecstatic. I immediately accepted.

One of these Sunday nights, I was surprised by a visit from my in-laws. After the service, my then mother-in-law told me something I will never forget. She said, "You've found your niche." I was so proud and honored. Talk about mountain top experiences, this was one. However, I would be soon taken down and by a preacher.

But not before many successes on those special Sunday nights. God poured out his spirit upon me and the youth every time. He was so faithful.

We would have the entire youth group fill the first four rows in the sanctuary. It was a wonderful experience to minister to kids who were open to learning how to follow Christ. Many accepted Christ during these special services. I'm sure the devil was angry, and he was anxious to destroy the works that were happening.

The church was located on a state highway with a lot boarded from the rear by a thick wooded area. I began to think this would be perfect for an outdoor drama. So I planned a "lock-in" for a Friday night. The kids were excited, and I believed God was going to do something special. And he did.

To prep the area for a live outdoor drama, my brother, my best friend, and I created a crucifixion set about five hundred yards into the woods in an area we had cleared. We planned to have the kids take a guided hike in the middle of the night down a candle lit path that would culminate at the scene. They would arrive at an opening and hopefully, be surprised to see a live enactment of the crucifixion complete with a man on the cross and a Roman soldier to narrate.

We started around 8:00 p.m. on that special Friday night. We had about seventy-six kids to attend. We had a blast eating junk food, playing, singing, and just hanging out. However, I explained to the kids that at promptly 3:00 a.m., we would all take a vow of silence and take a secret hike deep into the woods. They had no idea what to expect but were filled with anticipation.

As the 3:00 a.m. hour approached, we began the task of settling down more than seventy-five teenagers. Then one of the adult chaperons gave me the worst possible news. It was raining and raining hard. Everything will be ruined, I thought. The candles won't stay lit. Everyone will get soaked and become miserable. The impact would be significantly diluted.

I quickly gathered the chaperons for consultation. We all agreed that God had led us this far, so we must brave the rain and see what happened. And so we did. We issued each teenager a candle. We gave instructions that at exactly 3:00 a.m.; everyone would take a vow of silence. From that point, the group would be led silently into the woods in single file.

We slowly began the quiet journey into the woods. In the distant, we could hear the ringing of a hammer seemingly contacting some sort of iron or steel. The sound almost seemed amplified as it echoed through the woods. The rain continued but so did the hike. The closer to the opening we reached, we began to hear voices. The voices of men and the screeching sounds of a man groaning.

Not one time was it necessary to quieten the group. There was a deep and sacred silence that had fallen upon them. The sound of the rain falling through the trees and the sounds from the scene ahead held everyone spellbound. And slowly, the first hikers began to arrive at the opening and see the cross and the man nailed to it.

I had prepared a sermon that would end with an invitation to accept Christ. However, I soon realized none of my preparations were needed. The seventy-six or so teenagers gathered around the cross. I immediately noticed that the rain had created puddles of water and mud. Certainly, I could not ask anyone to kneel.

The Roman soldier addressed the group. He spoke boldly and scornfully. He ridiculed the man hanging on the cross. As he spoke to the group, I surveyed the crowd. Every eye was focused on the cross almost oblivious to the jeering of the soldier. It was the man on the cross who held them in total suspension.

Suddenly, the man on the cross lifted his head and spoke. "I did this for you," he said lovingly. My brother was playing the part so well. Of course, it was the anointing of the Holy Spirit. "All I ask is that you live for me," he continued. "Who will accept my gift of salvation?" he said with a deeper tone and booming voice.

Then I saw the most beautiful sight I have ever seen. One by one, teenagers began to kneel in the muddy puddles without being asked. They wept as they accepted Jesus Christ as their personal savior in the woods in a pouring down rain. Take that, Mr. Devil!

So how did I crash and burn after this magnificent success? Not to mention the terrific choir, the drama team, or the very successful fund raising. Things were going my way, all right. But I managed to do just that. Crash and burn…again.

The Pastor Who Missed the Mark

I believe Church people cause more people to go to hell than they influence to go to heaven. Most of my life I've observed the meanest, rudest, most self-centered, jealous, lying, and vindictive people are the ones who attend church regularly—the members. They are deacons, teachers, choir members, and even the pastors. These church members are self-appointed judges and juries.

If you don't believe in miracles, you will believe if you can find a preacher's kid who is successfully serving the Lord with a total commitment as an adult. This is a true miracle. If a kid can grow up in the cesspool called the parsonage where the stench that reeks day and night is inescapable and end up a Christian. Wow, what a miracle!

For the first twenty-nine years of my life, I was attacked emotionally on a regular basis. Somehow, I kept coming back for more. I would take the hit and react. And my reactions were always wrong. The irony was I was totally oblivious to both. I don't think I ever consciously realized what was happening to me and how I was responding.

The result was failure covered with the deception of strength. I pretended to be tough. I was outspoken and said what I thought which always ended up hurting my parents especially my dad. Church members are super ignorant. They can't determine who is speaking to them. I know this because everything I said represented the thoughts of my father. Of course, they did, right?

I protested that these were my words, but it made no difference to the ignorant hypocrites. They associated my every word and action to my dad. It was as if I didn't exist. I was made aware of this through scolding and whippings. The stress of being the assumed mouthpiece of the pastor is too stressful for any kid to bear.

To be fair, pastors are under extreme scrutiny concerning their children. Any deviation by their offspring is a direct reflection on the pastor's effectiveness. Congregations give them no slack. It was particularly hard on my dad. He was a young man only in his early thirties when I entered high school. And to make matters worse, I was his first born forcing me to set the pattern. For me, the expectations were just too high.

It was at the age of twenty-eight; I learned the hurt not only came from everyone in the pews, it came from the pulpit as well. I was the youth pastor of this thriving church where God was pouring out his blessings as indicated by the muddy and wet service at the foot of the crucifixion scene deep in the woods in the middle of the night.

The parents were thrilled with the activity of their youth. My pastor was elated. I remember my dad telling me during that time that my pastor was truly blessed to have the youth program he had. It was a compliment to me. But the regret in his voice was undeniable. He was thinking back on the time when I was his youth pastor. Why couldn't it have worked? I know it hurt his heart as it did mine that we couldn't work together. But I did have his support in the new and exciting ministry.

Although she never said, I believe my wife was happier during this time than any time in our marriage. And the reason, she could trust me; she saw my dedication. And she was seeing the results of my ministry.

She worked full time in a pharmacy and was trying to earn a nursing degree. All while raising our little five-year-old daughter. Of course, she couldn't attend every function, but I had her full support.

For me, it was euphoric. For once, I wasn't the preacher's son. The best part was the feeling that what I was doing was pleasing in God's sight. I could see his stamp of approval on every aspect of that ministry.

We had a great choir, about seventy-five members. We practiced every Sunday afternoon before the evening service. (We had

Sunday night services back then) The drama team met on Friday nights rehearsing the latest play I had written. On Wednesday night, I taught scripture to the kids. And all the while, we were having fund raising events to fund a trip to the Smokey Mountains to visit the great outdoor performance of *Unto These Hills.*

The kids worked very hard. They sold doughnuts on Saturdays among other things while helping to plan a carnival. The parents were wonderful in their support of every activity. They were completely fine with the purpose of the fund raising. The fathers helped build props for the carnival, and the mothers helped with the treats and prizes. In just six short months, we had raised about $3,000.

On the outside, it looked as if I had finally defeated the devil. I could see myself as a pastor sometime soon. However, my inward struggles continued. No one knew. I can't explain it, but I felt like a fake. I felt as if I was swimming against a strong current pushing me backward from any progress I seemed to make.

As a preacher's kid, even when grown, you believe there is no one to whom you can confide. First, they wouldn't understand. Second, the terrible feelings if shared would only make you look bad. So I was stuck. Not stuck in the church where I was thriving but stuck with my childhood baggage and the loneliness associated with not having a confidant.

The drive to perform, to live, to preach, to teach, to achieve was an overwhelming emotion. No achievement was ever good enough. And there was my past failures that could surface at any time if I could depend on the faithful as I usually could to remind me of what sins I had committed.

On one occasion, after my first divorce, I was settled in my dad's church. My only involvement at the time was playing trombone in the church band. I have played trombone since the age of eleven, and it was and still is something I enjoy. We had several brass players, and it was always great to play together.

On one occasion, we all walked off the platform as usual and entered a small room just off the platform where our empty cases were kept. We chatted as everyone put their instrument away. I was the last to leave spending more time than usual wiping down my instrument. As I was placing the trombone in the case, I noticed a small piece of paper lying in the bottom of the case.

Curious, I laid my trombone down on the floor and picked up the paper. My name was on it. I remember thinking someone must have left me a note. As I began to read, my heart began to break in a million pieces. Here is what I read:

"Frank, you are such a hypocrite. I know what you are doing, and God will get you for it. You can pretend all you want but I know, and others know too how bad you are. You better confess, or I will expose you."

The note was not signed. Apparently, a Christian coward wrote it. Someone in that very sanctuary that I was about to go into and sit down had written it. The room was locked until I opened it just before the service began, so someone crept in just before the service began to leave the nasty note.

The pain I felt at that moment was the worst I'd ever felt. Anger came later. But brokenness was all I felt at the moment. I barely remember entering the sanctuary. All I could think about was finding my mother. When I did, I wept on her shoulders. After telling her about the note, she took the note up to the pulpit to my dad. I don't remember the next sequence of events except my ex-father-in-law speaking in my defense to whom I was so grateful. I didn't deserve his loyalty. But I will never forget it.

But just before that, nothing but good things were happening, and yet in my most private thoughts, I saw myself going through the motions. I projected confidence, but inside, there was none. But I carried on hoping what was happening would eventually make me happy inside.

For periods of time, I was happy. Mostly, when I was immersed in the ministry. The busier I was, the better. So I kept very busy. I worked a forty-hour-work week with the utility company, but my heart was at the church. And every possible hour was spent there.

I didn't see what was coming next nor could I have even predicted such a change. My pastor called me and told me he had always wanted to pastor a church in Valdosta, Georgia, and he was swapping churches with another pastor there. What? Was he kidding? First, how do you just decide to swap churches?

This impulse, and that's what it was, was not God's will; history has validated that. It was the beginning of the end not only for me but ultimately for every single young person in the Royal Reflection's youth group. I was crushed and immediately informed him that I knew protocol for staff and therefore would resign.

"Oh no," he said. "I've spoken with the new pastor, and he is excited about what is happening here and does not want to interrupt the programs." With that, the pastor that supported and loved me was gone, and a new one was on the way. But the love and support would leave with the pastor. The new pastor would be very different.

Several weeks passed before the new pastor arrived. My phone rang on a Saturday, and it was a voice I'd never heard on the other end. It was my new boss, my new pastor, hopefully, my new friend. He asked if we could meet sometime that day at the parsonage. I agreed and was on my way almost immediately.

I knocked on the parsonage door, and the pastor answered. He was a stoic man about six feet tall, slender, and with thinning hair. He appeared to be in his late forties. I found him to be cordial but not warm. In fact, he did not greet me with a smile which I thought was unusual and even unbecoming of a pastor.

He was all business. He confirmed what he had told the former pastor concerning my stay and the programs. But he added an odd request. He said he was there to preach only, and that I should lead all the services. He would just sit on the platform and be ready when I was ready for him to preach. How weird, I thought.

I remember going home and sharing with my wife what the new pastor had requested. She too thought it an odd request. The entire short meeting was odd; I didn't feel welcome in the parsonage that had been my second home for the previous year.

The former pastor and his wife had opened their home to me and my wife. We often stayed with them on Sunday afternoon between services. We lived about thirty miles away, and this saved us the time and energy of having to make the drive twice on Sunday. They were warm and friendly and became like family to us very quickly.

I fondly remember the former pastor asking me sincerely one Sunday afternoon what he could do to support me more. More, I thought? How could he do more? He was there for me at every turn already. Other than my own father, he was the finest man I've ever known.

We were able to accomplish so much in a very short time because of his vision although his vision occasionally needed an explanation. For example, he found a completely worn out single-wide trailer and had it towed to the rear of the church. When he called me and told me he had a surprise for me, I had no idea it was a broken-down trailer.

He wanted me to come and see what it was; he was excited. I could hear it in his voice. So I drove to the church on a Saturday to see what the surprise was. As I was driving into the church parking lot, I didn't even notice the ugly trailer sitting halfcocked on the rear of the property.

I walked up to the parsonage which sat adjacent to the church. The pastor walked outside before I could knock on the door and motioned for me to follow him. We walked to the eastside of the parking lot near the wooded area, and there it was.

"What do you think?" he asked me excitedly.

"What is it for?" I asked inquisitively.

"It's your new youth building," he said proudly.

My first thought was, "You're kidding."

What he saw and what I saw was two very different things. I saw a single-wide trailer in terrible shape that wasn't worth anything and was useless. He saw a trailer transformed into a youth meeting hall equipped with surround sound, restrooms, and a small library.

He explained his vision. The youth would work on this "project" on Saturdays. First, we would need to gut the interior. Then we would begin the remodeling. "It will be a great team building project," he exclaimed. He was thrilled with his plan, and I didn't want to damper his spirits whatsoever, so I tried to be equally as positive. But looking at the heap of junk, it was difficult for me.

The outside siding was rusted and warped. The skirting was missing. The windows were broken out. The two doors were both damaged and barely hanging on the hinges. And if possible, the inside was worse.

The flooring was rotted away in most places. The odor was horrific. The walls were water logged. The electric wiring was hanging everywhere, and the heating and air duct system was completely missing.

But this was what I loved about this pastor. He was not moved by what he saw. Instead, he was moved by what he couldn't see but would see. He envisioned a beautiful youth hall that would serve as the nucleus for all our activities. He saw a starting point; a place to grow and develop.

The old trailer would be transformed into a place the youth could gather and grow spiritually. But that would be just the beginning. Later, we would build a huge multipurpose building that would contain all his dreams (and mine). It was not to be. His vision and mine would die very shortly with the arrival of the new leader.

The good pastor who was my support and friend left because he wanted a change. A few months after he left, he returned to visit me and my wife in our home. He was devastated over what had transpired since his departure. But it was too late. The vision had ended. The youth group was broken apart, and my marriage was next. All because two men swapped churches without seeking God's will in the matter.

That day sometime in late 1986 was the last time I ever saw or spoke to that special pastor. He retired at some point and returned to his childhood home about sixty miles from our special church. A few years ago, I heard he passed away and went to be with the Lord. The church where we both shared a very special ministry is no longer there as the same church. The people were scattered and only God knows what happened to all the young people.

It was the first Sunday for the new pastor. As requested by him, I led the service. At the appropriate time, I introduced our new pastor. And for the next month, that's the way the services would go. We had good services, and the new pastor was quite the preacher. And as far as preaching goes, he was better than my former pastor. But that's where the comparison ended. He was not supportive of me, and it was evident.

I could sense a tension between us from the beginning. One sign was his calling me, "Brother Gray" instead of calling me by my first name, Frank. Another was the changes he began to make. After three Sundays, he called me into his office before Sunday school began, and I couldn't imagine the hostility I was about to encounter.

He began by informing me that the parents were complaining that their teens were spending too much time at the church. If the kids participated in everything we offered, they would be at church four or five times a week. This was a first for me. I'd never heard of (Christian) parents complaining their kids were too involved in Church. Incidentally, I've never heard from or met any of these complaining parents to this day. The pastor lied, simply put.

He proceeded to tell me which activities would be cut and the frequency of the remaining. Worst of all, he had moved the funds we had raised for our trip from our youth fund to the general treasury and told me the trip was cancelled. I remember being completely flabbergasted. I sat silently for a moment to gather my thoughts and reached the only conclusion I could. I resigned. His response was cold and calculating. He just replied, "I thought that's what you would say."

He explained that my popularity was an issue and in fact, was greater than his own popularity among the congregation, so my resignation was for the best. This same pastor who had insisted on my leading all the services is now questioning who is more popular. The same pastor who was the envy of most pastors who would kill for a thriving youth group. But blatant jealousy blurred his vision.

In some twisted manner, he had thrust himself into a popularity contest with me which he thought I was winning. I certainly didn't think there was a contest; however, I was keenly aware that I was more revered by the congregation than he was. But it was his fault. He's the one who implemented the service pattern. And he's the one that was cold and unapproachable outside the pulpit. No wonder no one warmed up to him.

I left his office hurt and confused. I found my wife and gave her the news. She was extremely distraught and would not come into the sanctuary for the morning service. I felt I needed to attend my last service as the pastor had said he would announce my resignation during the service. I understood my wife's feelings, and she sat in the car for the duration.

At some point, the pastor announced my resignation and told the congregation I felt the need to move on to another ministry—another lie. But I respect the position of pastor and therefore, chose not to challenge what was being communicated.

There were many tears shed that morning from parents and teens as I left for good. But the damage was far more serious than I realized at the time. My ministry would end; my marriage would end, and my life would drastically change. But the greatest tragedy was the youth. As far I know, most walked away from church and never came back.

A few months after I left, the church held an election and voted to send the pastor packing. But it was too late to recover. The lies he told were convincing as he was the pastor and was presumed to be telling the truth. And I was not there to defend myself. Just two examples, he had told the leaders that I had refused to attend meetings with them, not true; he had said I had lost my license with the Assemblies of God, not true.

But the worst was yet to come. My wife did not believe I handled the situation correctly. We were both devastated and lost. All because of a decision to just swap churches. But the root problem was who I was. I was a preacher's son and had a target on my back. I didn't see the target and was unaware of the arrows or from what enemy from whence they came. I didn't see it and had a pastor who not only missed it too but missed the mark of the devil's work completely.

Stop the Cycle

More than thirty years after my ministry of youth ended, it occurred to me that all preachers' kids are born with a target on their backs. After all I've endured, the realization that it was never the deacons or church members was startling. Neither was it the high expectations or a glass house syndrome. And it wasn't peer pressure.

It wasn't even the hypocrisy so real in every church. The target is about stopping the cycle. I believe Satan has a battle specific plan to stop preacher's kids from continuing the ministry. Maybe, we are his number one enemies. Or better yet, maybe we are his greatest threat.

Think about it. If a kid can come through all the grime and dirt found in every parsonage, overcome all the unreal expectations, resist the constant urge to rebel, ignore the members scowling, and be oblivious to criticism, imagine what a force of ministry that would be. And Satan knows it.

Most preacher's kids that leave the church never come back to God. But the minority that do enjoy effective and powerful ministries. They relate with extreme grace and mercy. And their ministries are humble and grateful. They are aware of how far they fell away and of the amazing grace that brought them back.

I believe preacher's kids have the potential to shake the earth for God. Their heritage equips them with the power of the message second to none. No kid grows up with such a knowledge of the Lord outside of the preacher's home. If you're not a preacher's kid, you won't get what I'm saying. But if you are, you know the truth.

So what happens? It's simple. We are targeted. What I know, Satan knows as well or better. My dad is the most dedicated man I've ever known. He set his mind many years ago when he was very young. He decided to follow the call without any regard to anything that would prevent him from doing so. And at the time of this writing, he's still going strong at the age of seventy-eight.

My dad had three sons. Now, what if all three of us followed his example of dedication and unabridged faithfulness? Satan would then have four powerful warriors to fight against instead of just one. Four times the gospel, four times the power, four times the prayers, four times the effectiveness, four times the determination, and most importantly four times the ability to spread the Gospel of Jesus Christ to a lost and dying world. This extrapolation can apply to every single preacher and their offspring.

I wish I could say I stepped in Dad's footsteps, but I can't. Like hundreds of thousands of other preacher's kids, I didn't continue the cycle with any consistency until my light of ministry finally went out. For years, I blamed all the players in the church scenes. And I didn't understand what I had lost in terms of the cycle. Now, I do.

I'm not concluding that all preacher's kids are called into the ministry of preaching. However, I am suggesting that every preacher's kid is called to continue the cycle. God's master plan is discipleship. Why not apply this to the preacher's home? What greater discipleship program than that taught and experienced in the parsonage. Yes, the very same with all the dirt and grime.

I was middle-aged before I saw the parsonage as the training ground for battle against Satan. The parsonage I have resented for most of my life was the very same place I was recruited as a soldier and where I gained my training to fight. It was from that parsonage that scriptures came back to me that I don't remember studying on my own. It was from that parsonage that conviction ever compelled me to do the right and run from wrong.

It was from that parsonage that I learned I'm never alone in my darkest night. It was from that parsonage that I learned God is real and faithful no matter where my journey has taken me. And I can always come home no matter how far I've drifted. As can every preacher's kid whose life has gone astray.

Sadly, some preacher's kids never make it home because of the blurred lines between authenticity and counterfeit. Exposure to the true Gospel is skewed by everything opposite that is observed. The irony for a preacher's kid is the relative closeness to Christian principles and the few church members that practice the principles.

Seeing church members committing acts of obvious sins such as lying, cursing, cheating, or stealing rarely taint the reality of the Gospel in the hearts of preacher's kids. Gossiping, back stabbing, criticizing, and judgmental attitudes are the culprits and just bad attitudes in general.

Church members focus and feed on trivial matters—the color of carpet, how the money is allocated, who is placed in leadership, who sings or plays instruments—and throw in a building program and the church member demons come out. In the local church, the members fight each other and the pastor over just about any issue.

As a preacher's son, I have rarely, if ever, seen the true Spirit of Christ manifested in a church member. The Bible tells us that the tongue is the unruliest member of the body. And church members have less control of their tongues than most who never darkened the church doors. These uncontrolled tongues have split many churches.

I've never understood how a church splits. If Christians can't get along with each other, the Spirit of the Gospel is absent. How can a church member expect to gather their marbles and go somewhere else and receive God's blessings? I chalk it up to forgetfulness. They forget scripture such as the one that says we should dwell together in unity. And the scripture that says God hates those who sow discord among the brethren.

Restoration is another expectation from a Christian. A Christian should restore someone who has fallen. My experience is the opposite. On many occasions, I have been cut off. Being cast away does not bring repentance. Instead of repenting, most of us preachers' kids rebel.

I've heard the subject of the stoning of a sinful woman in the Bible preached many times. I've never seen the practice of restoration.

Remember, he without sin cast the first stone? Church members are expert stone throwers especially at preachers' kids. When a preacher's kid sins, the father or pastor often has the dilemma of explaining restoration. Why would you have to explain this Christian principle? Because if he tries to restore his own child, church members regard this as condoning the sin.

However, the church members' kids are exempt from condemnation. And here's why. They are not expected to be perfect. They have no image to protect. And even worse, the kid's sin is not a reflection of their failure as parents. But let a preacher's kid fail, and the assumption is the pastor has failed.

My bitterness often came from this very concept. When I was young, I was keenly aware that my every word and action was a direct reflection on my father's ministry. The response was rebellion. The pressure to act to protect my father was too much for me to handle. And I cracked under the pressure.

I was often caught between being favored because I was the preacher's kid if I was called on to do something and being the brat if I misbehaved. I remember the reaction to my middle brother's talented singing. The congregation was cold and never really responded. He had a great voice, but each time he sang, the reaction was the same. It seemed odd that he never received requests to sing while others who sang did. Why? Because he was the preacher's son.

I believe all these barriers and challenges are calculated by Satan. His objective is to discourage every preacher's kid so the cycle ends. Regardless of the scenario, Satan vividly points out all the flaws in the church when otherwise may go unseen.

The satanic plan is to pile on. And eventually, it all runs together, and truth is covered by what is seen and heard. I believe Satan calculates the pile on because no one thing alone could cause a preacher's kid to turn away. But the compilation drives the preacher's kids away permanently.

When the cycle ends, and a preacher's kid turns away, usually he or she turns with vigor. It's not enough to just drop church. The preacher's kid tries to go as far away as possible. This means to commit as many ungodly acts as possible. Hereby, comes the theory that preacher's kids are the worst.

Good news is some preachers' kids have continued the cycle. Some become ministers. Some become evangelists. Some go to the mission field. And some become faithful church members and work with a fervent dedication in the church. But it often follows rebellion and rejection.

Those who have not yet come home to their teachings are destined to live unfulfilled lives that will end in death and after death, judgement. No amount of *fame* and fortune will hide the truth each have been taught. No amount of success will heal the heart. A preacher's kid is doomed to know the truth without the ability to forget.

Proverbs 22:6 says, "Train up a child in the way he should go: And when he is old, he will not depart from it." There it is. You may not live for Jesus, but you will always have the knowledge no matter how far away you go from the scriptures. And there is danger ahead. To know it and not live it is dangerous.

All of us preacher's kids not only have the target on our back but the knowledge in our hearts. Luke 12:36 suggests a caution that much will be required of the person to whom much is given. Very few receive more of the scripture than preacher's kids.

It is very dangerous for a preacher's kid to stray from the scripture. Each that do so will be held accountable for all they were taught. But Satan knows the scripture even better and will try to deceive by forcing doubt. Is there really anything to the stuff you were taught? Maybe it all is just a farce that men have carried on. Doubt is conceived and born in this deception. The cycle stops. Satan wins. Next is the trophy case.

The Trophy Case

I don't know how many sermons I've heard my dad preach. Some I can remember, and many I can't. For example, I will never forget him announcing one Sunday morning that his sermon for the evening service would be, "The Pig That Got a Permanent Wave."

He did a masterful job explaining the story of "The Prodigal Son" and how he had ended up in the pig's pen. And there he lamented his condition and decided to go home and repent. It was then he made up his mind to wave goodbye to the pigs, permanently. Dad preached that sermon over thirty years ago, and it still resonates with me today.

However, the most impactful sermon I've ever heard is when my dad preached a sermon he called, "The Devil's Trophy Case." The message was simple and at the same time profound. He described each person that refused to accept Christ as a win for Satan whom he proudly displayed in his trophy case.

Trophies signify a win. However, the size and shape are not necessarily the indicators of the magnitude or significance of the win. But if I imagine that these were the indicators of the size or significance of the win, I would see Satan's trophy representing a preacher's kid as one of the largest in his collection.

Satan has sought my demise my entire life. And not just mine but every preachers' kid ever born. Sadly, many succumb to the torment, frustration, pressure, and disbelief. Honestly, though I've never denied Christ, I've had times where I questioned if all I had been taught was real.

I can only describe the torment in my mind as a tornado of thoughts swirling viscously in my mind. The only reason I survived is my parent's dedication in the home. I'm sure the devil hated the nightly routine. Before bedtime, Dad would call us all around the bed for scripture reading and prayer.

There were no excuses not to attend these sessions. If one of us were sick, the session would move from Mom and Dad's bed to the bed of whomever was sick. If friends were over, they were invited to join. I remember some did and others chose not to. But I was always embarrassed to say I had to go and pray.

Dad would read scripture and each of us boys had to say a prayer. At first, it was the favorite "Now I lay me down to sleep." But as we grew older, we had to say our own prayers. The time would end with a prayer from our mom.

I'm sure there must be other families who had the same routine, but oddly enough, I've never met them. In fact, I've never heard of one single family who did this with such regularity. Though he never said, I always assumed Dad made it his thing to do this and start it from the beginning.

I don't remember the first time, but I do remember each of my brothers being added to the routine. This continued until we left home. Even dating didn't interrupt the reading and prayer session. As the oldest, I began dating when both my brothers were still young. My curfew was ten o'clock. My brothers could not go to bed until I came home, and the reading and prayer could begin.

Dad didn't have a time frame to fill. He read a group of scriptures, maybe a chapter or so. Then we prayed short prayers, and that was it. And as I grew older, I didn't really pay attention to the reading. I was most likely ready to get back to TV or whatever else I was doing.

I didn't fully appreciate what was happening at the time or realize the eternal gift my dad and mom was giving us. It would be years later before I knew. However, my first realization came when I was attending Southeastern Bible College in Lakeland, Florida.

One night my roommates and I were studying and preparing for a test. We were quizzing each other with probable questions and topics. I was doing well. In fact, I was answering every question correctly. Frustrated by this, one of my roommates asked, "Did you learn all this at First Assembly in Savannah?"

I responded without thinking. "No, I said. I must have learned this at Bedside Assembly."

I can only conclude a direct correlation exists between the family prayer sessions, and the fact that my brothers and me all serve Christ today. We never became a permanent trophy in Satan's trophy case. I can't speak for my brothers, but it was close many times for me. I could have easily ended up there. But I didn't by the grace of God.

I would love to personally ask thousands of preacher's kids who have turned from Christ if they had a family altar. I'm guessing the majority did not. Most preachers preach from the pulpit in the sanctuary of the church. My dad did his most impactful preaching around the bed every night.

I could criticize my dad for many things; for putting the church members ahead of us many times; for not defending us against the members and especially deacons; for not being able to separate the pastor role from the father role; for being too strict; for not understanding the intense pressure to which we were exposed. But how could he know? He wasn't a preacher's kid himself.

But I know this one thing for sure. Dad did his very best as he saw it. And the things he and so many other preachers do that are wrong for their kids; he did the one thing right. He established the family altar. And I believe with all my heart and soul this one thing kept us from being one of Satan's trophies.

Satan has thrown his best tactics at me, and many have been successful. I've been beaten by him many times, but in the end, he will lose. And thanks to Dad and Mom and the family altar, he will never have me permanently in his trophy case.

But the tragedy and significance of the trophy case is the finality of the setting. Once a trophy is in the case, it represents a concluded timeframe or event. For Satan, the trophy is a symbol of not only a victory but a final defeat and a battle which never need be fought again. The basis is a theory that concludes that once a trophy is in the case, the place of abode is permanent.

Tragically, for many who become trophies of Satan, the permanent status is the reality. The case is locked, and like actual trophies, the trophies remain. However, the difference is Satan's case is a delusion. There are no locks. There are no obstructions from exiting. Furthermore, the trophies can dissolve. They are not real. They are only temporary holders for temporary victories. But the delusion is so compelling; the individual believes they are trapped.

For preacher's kids who fall victim to the trophy case, the outside holds no appeal. The relegation to the case is comfortable. No strife to maintain a standard is ever felt. No one attempts to knock the trophy from its position. And the inanimate status provides a sense of security. If I'm not moving, I can't be knocked off.

Satan's baffling attempt to subdue and defeat is wrapped up in his ability to lull someone into an inanimate state. All the while providing metaphorical successes to feed the innate need to become something other than a preacher's kid. In some cases, it's fame and fortune, but my experience is otherwise.

After each defeat, Satan would place me as a trophy in his case. He never offered or provided me fame or fortune. What he provided instead was acceptance. When I was in the case, I accepted that God was done with me. I accepted that I had misaligned my life with God's will and plan. Therefore, it was over for me in terms of ministry or service to him.

Regardless of what it takes for Satan to keep one in his case, he deals with the secret needs and fleshly desires to provide an accommodating environment. I often underestimated the power of Satan and his desire to have me. I ignored the signs and kept inflating my confidence and ego. He would use both against me in each battle, and he would win.

Why would Satan desire to have a preacher's kid in his trophy case any more so than any other kid? It's a slap in the face of God. He is ripping a part of the ministry out of the mainstream that he believes is God's domain. After all, his ultimate battle is not with humans; it is with God.

Satan rebelled and left heaven in opposition to God. He sees an opportunity for an inside hit when he attacks the preacher's home and offspring. He knows God called, and his servants answered. He may be ineffective in his influence on the ministers, but the children are innocent and become prime candidates for destruction.

I had many stints in the trophy case. But one I remember most was during the demise of my marriage. After the divorce was final, I remember feeling desolate. I said aloud, "Devil, you finally ended my last chance at ministry."

At twenty-nine, I was in his case and defeated. The trophies around me brought me no comfort. I was alone amongst others who fell before me. But was it over for me? Not entirely. That's when the mercy of God was revealed to me. True, I would not become a pastor. True, I would not ever be in full-time ministry again. But I realized in time, I was not completely done in.

The path would be modified just for me. Modified to accomplish something for God even in failure. God did not discard me for a new vessel. Instead, he chose to clean this old vessel and show his infinite love and power by restoring me for some use in his will. When I believed this, the trophy dissolved. I was set free from the case.

Preacher's kids are the worst. I get it. But why are they? Among many reasons I have and will record in this book is the trophy case. Beyond belief, like many preacher's kids, I took some level of pride when I became a trophy. I reveled in rebellion. The more I was pushed, the more I rebelled.

It's difficult to explain the sense of empowerment when indoctrinated in good yet transforming the good into acts of defiance. The difficulty resides in the spiritual and not the physical. Recognition of the difference is even more difficult. Satan's warfare tactics are spiritual and therefore, a fight for the mind and control of the thoughts.

A preacher's kid's mind has the blessing of infiltration of positive relational connections with God. This is the first contact point of the spiritual nature of the environment in which the kid dwells. The physical aspect and warfare is with the people with whom the preacher's kids associate.

Sadly, the battle lost most frequently is with the physical. Consequently, the spiritual battle succumbs, and the mind and thoughts are altered from the spiritual teachings. The result is the answer to why preacher's kids are the worst.

Speaking from experience, my thoughts were clouded by physical reactions to what my eyes and ears saw and heard. What I had been taught via scriptures paled to what I was feeling. I became weary of the fight to live by faith considering the pain inflicted by Satan through people.

Involuntarily, I became a trophy of Satan. I faced the dismal view from inside the case and the awesome feeling of disappointment with myself and my religion. Systemically, the blame morphs into defense and defense into doubt. I believe this experience defines and explains why preacher's kids are perceived the worst.

For preacher's kids, the road from religion to doubt is as short or long as the distance from the trophy case to the altar. And in many instances, the distance is too long to travel. Due to the burdensome journey, the intended destination of the altar becomes the unintended destination of disbelief.

Is It All Real?

Is there a God who directs the lives of men? Is there a God who answers prayer? Is there a God who is near and is involved in our lives? These are questions that would not be expected to be asked by a preacher's kid. But the reality is I've asked these questions and many more.

I was raised in a Pentecostal environment. I've seen what I know is the real moving of the Holy Spirit. I even saw a man run the tops of the church pews with his eyes closed and his hands raised. He never missed a step. I know this was miraculous and couldn't have been done except under the guidance of the Holy Spirit.

Of course, some would call such a display ridiculous. Maybe, holy rolling, but I saw it with my own eyes. When he completed what could be called a circus act, he fell limp behind the last pew. When he got up, he was not hurt at all. How was this possible?

I've prayed over an old worn-out washing machine that was stopped and smoking. I couldn't afford a new one and believed as I laid my hands on the old machine. I witnessed a miraculous occurrence as the machine began to work and continued working with no smoke until I could afford a new one.

After my first divorce, I had an old car with a cracked block. I couldn't afford to buy another car or have the engine replaced. Once again, I laid my hands on the engine and asked God to let it run normally until I could replace it. I drove the car another two years without issue.

Many times, I've seen the power of God in my life yet doubt still crept in like a mighty sea with waves crashing over my head. I would succumb to the waves and be knocked down repeatedly. A lot of years would go by before I realized what the evangelist had said to me was happening. I was being sifted like wheat.

To make matters worse, for every example of the reality of God came many more examples of false religion and hypocrisy. This caused me to think maybe the examples were mere coincidences. I saw people supposedly become Christians only to return to their previous lives. And I saw self-proclaimed Christians never leave their previous sinful lives.

Maybe, it's all about emotion. Just like at a football game where everyone jumps and yells and even cries at the outcome, win or lose. There is no divine force involved. Just raw emotion based on a passion. I'm very emotional, and I've often thought that's all there was to this religious experience.

And who is right? Different denominations have different interpretations of how it all works. How do I know the way I was raised is the right way? Are there many ways that lead to the same conclusion? And then comes the biggest question of all. Are you always saved if you were once saved as a kid? Is it true that once we are saved, we are always saved?

The overwhelming and innate sensation is to run. Get away from everything in the church. The confusion, conflict, hypocrisy, and all the debates leave a distaste in every preacher's kid's mouth. There is a thirst for escape. And hereby begins the negotiations with God.

I will leave the church but not God totally. I will not be suppressed by the teachings that cannot be proven to be effective or even legitimate. I will go my own way but will not let go of God. I don't need church. I don't need a regimented activity or involvement in the church. I need to express myself outside of the prison bars of my parent's beliefs and the church. If there is a God, he will understand, and he knows my heart.

The problem with this thought process; it doesn't ever work. Complete peace never comes, and bitterness is unmanageable. God simply does not negotiate with people. It's his way or no way. Therefore, a preacher's kid who chooses to leave the teachings will ultimately be self-exiled to a life of discontent misery. And there is no escape.

The void is often filled with worldly successes. Even riches in some cases are attained. Talent, skills, and other attributes learned in the church are transferable. The devil is a willing participant and will work with anyone to provide a path to happiness and fulfillment. Problem is he doesn't say how it ends.

The God-given talents to many preacher's kids are used in every way that is disconnected from the giver. But God never intended to have these talents wasted. And he won't compromise the use of these talents.

But what about the blessings? True. One can be very successful with the talents used for the world. But these are not blessings. These are just results or obtainment of goals. As a preacher's kid, the temptation is to exploit any talent just to prove it's possible to be successful away from the church. And it does work in many cases.

But what does it get us to be famous or notably successful? I've never been famous, but I have been successful in a secular job. I'm educated and enjoy a nice salary and benefit package. But I'm haunted by what could have been. Good news is I'm convinced the mercy of God allows for adjustments to his plan when we foul it up. But still we must adjust to the new plan if we expect to be whole.

As a preacher's kid, I cannot escape the question of whether it's all real. But this is me. No other preacher's kid was interviewed for this book. I have done absolutely no research. But brashly, I'm convinced my story will resonate with every single preacher's kid who reads it.

What is real? For me, life outside of service to God is an alternative universe that has no reality. That is real. The disciple Peter must have felt the same emotion. When asked by Jesus if he would follow suit with everyone else and leave, Peter answered, "Where would I go?" He discerned a spiritual profundity. No one, including hurt, damaged, and bitter preacher's kids have another option.

But preacher's kids run away with great intensity. I know because I tried when I was younger. The question is where does one run? To whom does one run to? To what solution other than Christ does one ever attain?

This is what I have resolved in my mind and heart. Why would I sacrifice a relationship with the one who loves me the most, supports me the most, and will never leave me for some lame reasons such as church member hypocrites? I don't let hypocrites keep me from eating at my favorite restaurant. I shop at the malls with liars, adulterers, pedophiles, rapists, murderers, and every sort of evil person. Yet I make my purchases without hesitation.

What is real? The confusion between spiritual reality and the deceit. I was exposed to spiritual reality from infancy. As is the case for all other preacher's kids. So how does the road lead away and when does the alternate path become enticing? The beginning is rooted in a natural human emotion, hurt.

I will never believe a preacher's kid decides to abandon his or her teachings at five years old. Nor does any other kid. So when do they? There is no set time or age. It occurs after accumulation of hurt experienced from other church goers. I was in my twenties before the weight of hurt finally began to impact my life.

Suddenly, while in my mid-twenties, I was convinced the church wasn't working for me, and I could get out while holding on to my belief in God. I laid the blame on the church members for my sins. They were the ones who bruised me. They were the ones who lived to see me suffer. Most importantly, they were the ones who consistently accused me. Why not just do the things of which I am being accused, I thought. I finally did.

The disdain I had for church members was exceeded only by my disdain for the devil. Had it not been for the mercy of God, I would have let church members cause me to continue to question the reality of religion. After all, most church members have no clue as to what religion is. And I mean religion by the Bible's description.

The Bible says that "pure religion" is visiting the fatherless and homeless. If you're a church member reading this, did you know that? I doubt it. If you do know it, why are you not practicing "pure religion?" Of course, as a church expert (which preacher's kids most definitely are), I can say I have *never* met a church member who practiced "pure religion" per the Bible's description. How sad.

It's no wonder preachers' kids question the reality of the Gospel experience. But are the church members totally responsible for this outcome? I wish I could blame it all on them, but the diversion from the church is all on us preachers' kids. Regardless of the lack of pure religion, we have no excuse. We are all accountable because of the exposure. Not to all that is wrong in the church but to all that's right in the "real" church which is the Bride of Christ not made of brick and mortar.

So what does it all mean? For me, it's simple. The Gospel is real. Jesus is real. He shed his real blood on a real cruel cross. He died on real cross and was placed in a real tomb. He rose again with a real body. He ascended into heaven to a real father. And he is coming back for a real church, for the real Christian. No one will ever convince me differently.

But at times, I lost sight of the "real Church" as I would suppose happens to other preachers' kids, as well. The Body of Christ is the "real Church" but only a small portion of it exists in any one congregation. Therefore, the view from the parsonage is skewed. This became evident to me as a young adult.

I viewed the church as a body of believers in a specific place or places. I certainly knew there were many Christians around the world and not just in my own church. However, I viewed my local church as a group. This was a mistake. It wasn't a group at all. The fragments of the real church existed in single numbers. There were only a small percentage that were practicing Christians in my church.

Later, I understood that it was likely that very few Christians existed at all in my church other than my parents. Mostly, the others were just pretend Christians. Not many reflected the love of Christ. Not many emulated his mercy and grace. Not many supported me; most ridiculed me.

The Mind of Christ that the Apostle Paul spoke about to the Philippians was never a part of the fabric that wove our congregation together. Here is how I know for sure. The Mind of Christ does not divide. Yet we had divisions. The Mind of Christ doesn't promote criticism and gossip. Yet we had both. The Mind of Christ would not resist the leadership of the pastor. But we had plenty resistance.

The Mind of Christ does not insert selfishness. Yet most of the members were selfish. Their main concerns were if the pastor appreciated them or visited them or gave them some sign of recognition. Their priorities included making sure their voices were heard, and the deacon board was making the best decisions. They were, after all, tithe payers who had an investment. What a joke!

Paying tithes and offerings is not a membership fee and has no intended or unintended rights or say so. For those who think so, they are giving for the absolute wrong reason. That too is not the Mind of Christ.

The Mind of Christ restores those who have fallen. Yet our church members sought punishment even to the point of restrictions or Christian timeouts. How hypocritical it is to insist someone cannot be used on the platform because of sin. What a demonic scheme.

The assumption that someone cannot be used on the platform because of sin in their life is beyond ridiculous. Does it mean that the ones who believe this are without sin? Or better yet does it mean their sin is of lesser impact?

The Mind of Christ doesn't care who gets the credit as the job gets done. However, I've seen church members quit or fail to complete a job because they were not appreciated. The Mind of Christ in a musician or singer sings for the glory of Christ. Most of the singers I've heard sang for self-gratification. How do I know this? I saw their reaction when a period passed, and they were not called on to sing, not the Mind of Christ at all.

The only conclusion I can draw is most church members are only Christians by name classification. They exhibit none of the attributes of Christ. They are a dichotomy of the fundamentalism of the New Testament.

Surprisingly, I still believe in the reality of religion. I believe salvation is real. I believe a close walk with Christ is real. And I believe in a real God who ministers to my every need every second of every day. My journey of enlightenment has been long but deliberate. I have fallen many times. And I've seen more than my share of church fakers.

Normality

I was married to my first wife for just over ten years. It's a wonder she lasted that long. Shortly after the divorce was final in March of 1988, I held hope that we could reunite. But it was not to be, and I don't blame her. Why would she trust me? I had never given her a reason to do so. She was more than ready for a new life, and she deserved a better one than the one I had given her.

I was fortunate that she was not a vengeful person. In fact, she left me the house and most of the furniture. What small amount of money we had, she left also. She moved into her new home with my daughter almost immediately. She intended for my daughter and I to have a close relationship and did everything possible to ensure we would. But divorce is so hard on kids. My daughter was only six years old at the time, and I'm sure the upheaval was much harder on her than her mother and I could admit. And things were about to get even harder.

My wife and daughter moved to Charleston, South Carolina, which is about 110 miles from Savannah. However, my weekends and times didn't change; only the drive was longer, about two hours longer. But I was determined to stay close with my daughter.

My wife was more than gracious with my times, and in the worst of scenarios, we worked together harmoniously for the first time. Of course, there were some bumps along the way, but I'm so thankful my wife never kept me from my child. She encouraged our times together, and I am forever grateful.

Over the next four years or so, we both remarried. My second marriage was a complete disaster and only lasted a couple of years. I'm not blaming my second wife. The failure was due to the marriage not being God's will for either of our lives. My first wife's second marriage also ended. I don't know the reason, but I felt bad for her. However, she did have two more children (which had been her desire) who are grown today and are terrific people. She was always a good mother.

When my daughter was sixteen, she moved in with me. I was thrilled, and for the first time felt like a "real" father. But I had a lot to learn. My first task was to teach her to drive. She was a good student and learned quickly. However, my most important task was to live a life before her that would influence her to follow Christ.

The years passed quickly, and before I knew it, she was moving out to start out on her own. I treasure the eight years we had together, and it laid the foundation for what we have today. She is now in her late thirties, and we are very close. We have standing Sunday lunches, and I always look forward to her coming over.

Unfortunately, as any child of divorce, she doesn't know the comfort of having parents living together and providing a loving home. There is nothing I can ever do to make up for that. But she knows I'm always here for her and will always put her first above any other person or thing.

She not only experienced her parents' divorce but was an innocent bystander for her parent's failure in a second marriage. Divorce is bad no matter what the circumstances, and no child should ever have to deal with struggle. While she has never said, I know she bears the scars for our mistakes.

In Satan's attempt to destroy me and her mother, she was collateral damage. There are so many things I would change if I could go back, but the effect on her would be the first. The irony is she should have been a preacher's kid. Although I know how hard that would have been, we will never know how that would have changed her world.

What I am most thankful for regarding my precious daughter is she knows the Lord. It hasn't been ideal, but she has made the right choice against the odds. My prayer is that somehow amongst the rubble, she has seen a change in me and knows how much I love her and want the best for her.

What I lost was the opportunity for her to see me in the role to which I was called. She has never known me in ministry. She was far too young to remember the time when I was temporarily successful as a youth pastor. As any child of divorce, my daughter was robbed of a stable home with two parents.

Her life was very different than mine. I had grown up with two Christian parents who loved each other and loved me. It's heartbreaking that she never experienced the home as God intended it to be. Her "norm" was altered forever when her mother and I divorced.

When the devil assaults and creates a casualty, the remnants of the struggle act as shrapnel and spreads to anyone near. Neither my daughter or I will ever know what could have been. She took the shrapnel, and I hate it. Although she never looks back, I know her heart has been impacted.

I regret that I did not see how my decisions would affect those I loved so dearly. As a preacher's kid, I should have been keenly aware of the devil's tactics and overall plan. He is only satisfied with destruction. One would assume incorrectly that fighting the devil for a long period of time would create a lack of tolerance for his evil and build a wall of defense against his weapons. If not careful, the opposite occurs. Blindness happens.

Once the devil is successful in blinding an otherwise clear vision, corrected vision is nearly impossible to achieve. For any preacher's kid who left the church and has never returned, the blindness continues. Satan will never allow the blindness to clear so that the preacher's kid can return home.

After a time, and it's different for every individual; the brain is convinced the former path is not possible or even desired. Have you ever heard, "Even if I wanted to, I couldn't?" A wayward preacher's kid heart is consumed with a sickness. There is no fever, no physical pain, no significant signs but sickness nonetheless.

This sickness is almost always denied. A wayward preacher's kid would probably never admit they have a sickness. But they do. They're sick of all the pain and hypocrisy. They're sick of all the rejections. And the sense of freedom feels like wellness.

As for me, during my wayward times, I felt vindicated. I felt strong. No one could make me do anything. I could choose my own path even if it was a far cry from my rearing. But repeatedly, I would find the strength I felt was a diversion straight from hell. I was not strong at all; I was extremely weak.

Like Samson in the Bible, I thought I could rise with power regardless of my indiscretions. But the name of Jesus is not a wildcard that can be pulled when in trouble. And the power from almighty God will not rest upon a wrong heart. He will not bless and prosper evil and bitterness.

Rebellion moves one further from his presence. He will not tolerate even a broken spirit if that spirit is one of a rebel. One who chooses to do their own thing despite what God's word says. Preachers' kids are prime examples of attempts to rebel from the teachings of the church.

However, the teachings of the church from God's word are not optional. One cannot create parallel routes with the objection of reaching the same destination. The routes chosen may be similar, but similar is not good enough. The route one chooses to take must be the route God has ordained. No substitute road will ever lead to his purpose or his blessings and most importantly, never lead to his anointing.

I'm an experienced traveler to foreign lands, not to France or Africa, never to Europe, never to South America, never to the West Indies. But where I've traveled is foreign land because it was not God's way or place. Anytime I chose not to find my way back to God's calling for my life, I was traveling in a foreign land.

I can describe the foreign lands to which I've traveled. Any joy found in these places was superficial and temporary. The people I met had no interest in my spiritual wellbeing. I found no fulfillment in any of these places. Satisfaction and contentment were absent. And peace was unattainable and distinctly bitterly missed.

I'm certain that no preacher's kid will ever find their success in a foreign land of which I speak. A land where prayer is a nighttime watch over me request. A land where Bible reading is a scant memory. A land where associates are as far from God as one can be.

I decided at some point to embrace my past not to accept it but to avoid repeating it. To do so meant to revisit the many miles I've traveled. What I discovered is God does not finish with us unless we finish with him. In his omnipotent power, he has followed me the many miles even when I drifted off his path.

Learning from the past is not a healing for me. In fact, it remains bitter and painful. The difference is hope for the future. And this hope in him who had never forsaken me will lead me some way, someday, to his intended place for me to be. Until then, I need to be careful. I need to make sure my will succumbs to his every single day.

Over twenty years have passed since my second divorce, and I am determined to never marry again. Too many people outside of the husband and wife are hurt when the marriage doesn't work out. I'm not willing to take that chance again.

Over this period, I've had years of reflection. Mostly, to understand what caused my life to collapse. Thus, the purpose of this book. I don't presume to believe I can be of any help to preachers' kids who are still living at home. What could I say to them to help them anymore than if some old preacher's kid would have said to help me. I wouldn't have listened or even understood. Plus, the times have changed, and I don't begin to understand how to communicate effectively to millennials.

Therefore, this book is meant to give hope to preachers' kids who are grown like me but have left God and have yet to return. And to help church members understand their roles in the lives of impressionable young preachers' kids.

This book is a fragment of the story of my life. I don't presume to think it's worthy of any sort of notoriety. I haven't reached any level of notable success nor does my story include elaborate or interesting drama that would be intriguing to anyone. In fact, compared to other books about someone's life, this one would pale in comparison as far as a riveting read.

My life would simply be considered normal. Or would it be? What is normal? I'm no expert, but I do know normal is relative. Which means that normal means many things to many people.

What is normal to one person may be far from normal for another. But normality or lack thereof certainly shapes lives.

For many years, I have wondered what the reasons were for preachers' kids growing up and leaving the church. Naively, I have hoped that writing my story would somehow address those reasons as I recorded my experiences. One could derive from my experiences causal factors which might include parents being too strict or expectations being too high and unachievable and church members' actions causing the separation from religion. But is it really any of these things?

Maybe the Satanic influence and home interruption is the only reason. After all, any diversion from the truth comes from the evil persuasion. All lies and deceptions come from Satan. It is his entire mission to lead everyone away from the Gospel. So preachers' kids are just his victims as are anyone he leads away from Christ.

Based on what we read in the Bible and what our parents have told us, it's accurate to say, Satan is the culprit. But how does he pluck the kids with the most spiritual knowledge out of the hands of God? If this question can be answered, we would know what causes preachers' kids to stray.

Preachers' kids are raised in a cocoon of spirituality. In the preachers' homes, God is a familiar being. We learn who he is. We learn how to pray to him. We are taught his attributes. We are divulged in his Holy Word. Unlike most homes, God is the centerpiece. Now, I realize other homes are God-Centered. But the difference is the focus.

For any other homes, the focus is the livelihood of the parents, the education and care of the children, and the day-to-day customary activities. Church is a part of the family but not a part of everyday life. It's not that church is not important; it's just not the most important thing.

Here is a picture of a preacher's home. In a preacher's home, nothing trumps the church or any of its functions. The preacher rarely if ever calls in sick. The preacher doesn't really have an off day even though some preachers attempt to designate a day sometime during the week. Consequently, even on the designated day, the preacher is only off if he receives no calls for help.

A death in the church family will interrupt a day off. An illness requiring hospitalization of a member (or anyone a member knows) will cause the preacher to cancel his plans. Someone who is depressed and needs to speak with the preacher will not wait for another day. And the church members resent him not doing something as simple as answering the phone when they call regardless of his "off" day.

This differs from other Christian homes. When the mom and dad are off from their secular jobs, they are not expected to work. They can distance themselves from the job place and even turn their phones off. They have sick days and vacation days. Receiving a call from the place of employment to come in because another employee is sick would be considered odd.

The preacher's job is the church. He is expected to be there when he is sick, tired, depressed, broke, angry, happy, sad, hurt, or any shape he may be in. The relevancy of his situation is not respected. I've even heard church members declare that they pay him, and that's why he should be there.

I must stop here on that one. It is true that the preacher is paid by the membership. But if you think that's what drives any preacher to the pulpit Sunday after Sunday, you would be grossly incorrect. For a man called by God to the ministry, it is the calling that drives the passion to continually preach the Gospel. The salary is a necessary evil, and the preacher does not need it or desire it if he is truly a man of God. Take away the salary, and he will still preach until his last breath.

I'm tempted to speak to the millionaire preachers who do not fit the description I've just given. These are not pastors of small flocks where the ministry impacts lives at the rudimentary level. These are money-seeking manipulators who prey on the undeserving but gullible listeners who are foolish enough to support their worldly desires of wealth and statue. These preachers have large congregations and usually costly television ministries. Not to mention large staffs that do most of the laborious tasks, so he can "study' in his lavish office.

Try calling them when you are sick. Try calling them when you need someone in the middle of the night to come to your bedside or hold your hand in prayer over a child in despair. Try calling them when your marriage is collapsing. Try calling them when you've lost your job and don't know from where the next meal will come.

You will be lucky if you can get one of their high-paid staff members. And the likely response may be that you need to make a monetary sacrifice for your condition to improve. However, you will be placed on a prayer list. Okay, so I gave in to my temptation to blast the false prophets.

Back to the differences between the preacher's home and just a Christian's home. When company comes calling, church members miss church without hesitation. In a preacher's home, the company either goes to church with them or waits at home until the preacher returns.

When school activities conflict with church services, the church members give priority to the school activities and just miss the church service. But in the preacher's home, the school activities succumb to the higher priority of the church service. Neither the preacher or his kids miss church for any reason.

So now the question of normality. Which is more normal, the preacher's home or the Christian's home? The answer would depend on who you ask. However, I would like to attempt to answer this question from a preacher's kid's perspective. You may be surprised at my answer. Subsequently, I will present a case that says this issue of normality may be the root cause of a preacher's kid's spiritual departure.

The Preacher's Home Not Normal

From my seat in the house, there was absolutely nothing normal. To start, it wasn't even our home. It was the parsonage. The house belonged to the church and was part of the salary package for the pastor. And with that came many abnormal activities.

For example, the house also served as a counseling facility. Over the years, I remember many times being sent to my room because someone needed my mom and dad to talk and pray with them. Maybe, it was a marital problem or possibly a financial issue. It could have been anything from the serious to the petty, knowing church folks. But our privacy was invaded.

The house also served as a hotel for evangelists. And we had our share. Of course, my job would be to entertain the evangelist's kids. Sometimes, this was an easy task, and other times, it was unbearable. I thought some of these kids were brats. But what I didn't realize at the time was they were in an even worse arena than I was in. At least, I wasn't moved from pillar to post.

Like me, they were expected to exhibit perfect behavior. Although, again like me, they were unsuccessful at delivering. In retrospect, I can see tons of resentment demonstrated in their behavior. They were coping with an even more abnormal lifestyle than I.

I learned in their travel; they didn't always stay in a nice home with the pastor and his family. Often, they stayed in makeshift bedrooms in some part of a cold dark church or in less than desirable hotels. And even sometimes in the homes of members they had never met. Their accommodations also included eating at the mercy of the church members. And they never knew what the next meal would bring. They may receive a delicious meal or one not so tasty. But they must not complain. It was all part of the ministry—just normal.

As a preacher's kid, I never felt or sensed any separation from the church to the parsonage. That's where normality evaporates. In many ways, living in the parsonage is like being in church all the time. One might conclude that to be a good thing. But even Jesus didn't live in the church. Of course, he lived with the church in his heart, but he had a secular life with his mother and father.

To actuate the separation of church and home, when Jesus was twelve years old, he was teaching in the temple. When his parents found him, he was instructed to go home with them even though he protested and said he must be about his father's business.

Every kid needs a home that is a sanctuary of protection. And that home needs to be separated from the church. The church and home are two very separate places. And each should serve a specific need. When the two mesh together, the results are catastrophic. And by that, I mean kids leaving the Gospel and deciding not to serve God in their adult lives. Which is what this book is about.

God wonderfully made us with minds and bodies that must cohabitate in a healthy environment. I believe God expects us to be well-rounded. The restrictive environment of the church/home does not allow for balance. As a result, resentment and bitterness are born.

I'm suggesting the preacher's home is not normal. Furthermore, I'm suggesting the preacher's home may be the central cause of spiritual departure later in the preacher's kid's life. More than the church or its members, I believe the home may be the most powerful unintended consequence for departure from God. If this is correct, who's to blame?

Well, there's plenty of blame to go around. Or maybe blame is not the word that best describes the consequential results from living in the parsonage. The best word may be, accountable. Thus, who is accountable for the pastor's home not being normal? Both, individuals and groups, are accountable.

The first group is the parents or pastors. It would seem simple, even normal, that the parents would strive for a normal home for the benefit of their children. The fact is the parents are clueless. After all, they are called into the ministry. Everything else just falls in place. What the parents miss is they are called into the ministry, but the children are not.

However, in the defense of the parents, they had no training and in many cases were not preachers' kids themselves and therefore, just simply didn't know. They assumed the entire family was called. This is a devastating miscalculation. And it is what I call, "forced ministry."

I do not blame my parents in the least; I will always give them the utmost credit for doing the best they knew to do. Without ever asking, retrospectively, I'm confident they would have done things differently had they known the pressure my brothers and I were always feeling. I will say more about my parents in the final chapter and give them the respect and honor they richly deserve.

So the kids are not called into the ministry. They are "born" to those who are called. I believe this understanding could be the key to avoiding a lifetime of woe. However, I emphatically believe the kids are to be trained in the ways of the Lord just as any other kid should be. A misunderstanding of the two concepts will disable my ability to present a counter-active balance in my discussion of the preacher's home.

I believe the first step is open and honest communication. And I don't mean some modern-day hooey phooey self-expression. To me, child self-expression is just a crutch for insubordinate behavior. Children are not mature enough to breach self-expression from any depth perspective. Remember, "it's all about me" is the mantra for all children.

Subsequently, the open and honest communication of which I speak must be born in the love of God and the love of the parents. The parents are accountable to listen to the degree they can sense the root meaning of what the kids are trying to say without being condescending and obtuse.

Pastors must not only provide a family altar but also provide a family table. There are stark differences between the two. The critical family altar is meant to be a one-way communication from the parents to the children from the scriptures to introduce God and his relevancy to the kids. This will lay a foundation for why the parents are doing what they are doing in terms of their pastoral work.

The family table, on the other hand, is the non-spiritual arena in which the conversations should not be spiritually centered, and the discussion should not be on the church. The family table should be the centerpiece for the home's normality.

No degrees are needed on how the conversations flow. As with the family altar, the parents should take the leadership role. The parents must be intuitive at this all-important family gathering. And they must possess a high level of investigatory skills. This is important as it relates to how the conversations should begin.

And of course, the conversation should always begin with parents asking prodding questions to open the floor for discussions. I don't ever remember my dad or mom asking me how things were going at school. If they had sensed the need to inquire, just maybe they could have understood.

For example, when we first moved to Savannah in the summer before my seventh-grade year, my dad intended to sign me up for band to play the trombone. This would be a great challenge since everyone else in the band would have been playing their instruments for two years during the fifth and sixth grades.

There was a reason why I was a late comer. Back in Dublin, Georgia, beginner's band was offered for fifth graders. The entrance qualification consisted of receiving lessons on a small black flute type instrument. I failed the assessment and therefore, was not able to join the band and begin playing the trombone.

My dad is a piano player and had played the sousaphone in the band during his high school years. He had high expectations for me to follow him in music. Which I wanted to do as well. I don't remember exactly why, but I knew I could not tell my dad that I had failed the music test. Maybe it was the fear of disappointing him or maybe just fear of him in general.

So whenever he would ask about the band, I would lie and say something to the effect that it had not started yet. And the subject would come up frequently especially at the family altar anytime he read from Psalms where any instrument was mentioned. After reading, he would look up and ask me if I had heard anything. I would always lie and say, no. To my astonishment, even now I find it hard to believe that he was fooled. But he was throughout the entire fifth grade and most of the sixth.

I covered my deceit at every hand. In the fall of 1969, my best friend and I was school patrol guards at one of the crossings. After the thirty-minute assignment, we would ride out bikes home. Different from me, he had passed the music test and oddly enough, was learning to play the trombone. And his trombone was lying along with our books at the crossing.

Suddenly, my dad's car drove up, and he seemed upset. "Frankie, get in the car, hurry," he said. I quickly grabbed my books and noticed the trombone case. I did not want my dad to see it if he hadn't already. So I quickly hid it behind a bush. I got in the car and heard the news that my granddaddy, Dad's dad, had passed away in Atlanta, and we were headed to Macon where the funeral would be held.

My dad never mentioned seeing the trombone case. I'm sure he was distracted by the news of his father's death. I was certainly glad for the distraction as morbid as that sounds. Looking back, I wonder what my friend must have thought about me hiding his trombone case or if he saw me do it or if he had a difficult time finding it. He never mentioned it as I recall. It all worked out, I thought.

My dad was famous for repeating a quote from the Scottish Novelist, Walter Scott, from the seventeenth century. "O, what a tangled web we weave when first we practice to deceive." I have found no truer statement that this. Every time I've lied and attempted to deceive, the truth always came out. The failed music test was no exception.

Just after midyear of the sixth grade, somehow my dad had enough of my excuses and decided to meet with my teacher. Of course, he was told the truth. What is so important to me about this story is his reaction. As expected, he was angry. But his anger quickly turned to resolution. To me, he became an idol at that moment and taught me an invaluable life lesson about resilience.

He demanded to meet with the band director. I'll never forget that meeting on many levels. First, the meeting was not in a room or office. We met in the hall at my elementary school. Not sure why but assume the band director had to come there, and the hall worked.

He was a gruff heavy-set man who did not smile and did not warmly greet my dad. My dad firmly expressed his disappointment in the testing process and concluded it was unfair. Furthermore, the test on the flute could not possibly be an indicator of any potential or lack thereof, to play the trombone. The band director disagreed and defended the test.

Ignoring that Dad had told him I wanted to play the trombone, the director looked at me and asked me what I wanted to play. Of course, I responded, the trombone. Then a last impression that more than fifty years later still resonates with me occurred. The director said, "Son, you will never play a trombone. You don't have the skills."

The meeting ended, and my dad and I went home. On the way home, the conversation centered around my options in music but never included defeat. My dad wasn't willing to take no for an answer. I was impressed with his confidence and applied this firm determination to many of my life's scenarios.

Neither of us knew at time that in just a few short months, we would both start fresh in a new place. And Dad was not about to miss the opportunity. Sometime that summer, he must have contacted the band director at the new school in Savannah. Not surprisingly, he tried to convince the band director to let me in the band even without the previous two years of lessons.

I didn't hear the conversation and don't know if it occurred in person or on the telephone, but this I do know; the outcome was very different. I was allowed in the band with the stipulation that my dad would rent not buy a trombone. And the band director would assess my ability mid-year to determine if I could catch up with everyone else and continue in the band.

Now back to the family table. The school year began, and the first day was over. I got off the school bus with trombone in hand excited to tell Dad how the first day had gone and how I liked the band director. He and my mom and brothers had just returned home, and he was very upset about something church related.

"Dad, I shouted. Guess who my favorite teacher was today?"

"Put your things away and do your homework," he snorted back to me. I was devastated, but he never knew. After all we had gone through, he was not interested in the least about my first day in the band. Whatever the church issue was had taken precedence. This scar remained for years to come.

The first band director was proved wrong. I did learn to play the trombone and played in various college bands and orchestras. I was chosen to play with the White House Military Band in my hometown for a patriotic concert. Even though I was grown, I was so proud that my dad was there to see and hear it. During intermission, I reminded him of the band director years before who had predicted doom on my ability to play the trombone. We both laughed. But it was my dad's tenacity that secured that moment. I am forever grateful!

In later years, I also learned what caused my dad's response that first school day. He had been summoned to one of the deacon's homes. The deacon lived near the church and had a wood shop adjacent to his home. Upon his arrival, the deacon began to rail Dad about his visitation hours. I don't know the specifics, but I guess that whatever Dad was doing regarding visitation was not enough to please the deacon.

Almost half a century later, this incident still has a sting. First, the cranky ole deacon had verbally attacked my dad unmercifully and second, consequently, ruined my first day of school. This is another example of deacons/church members negatively impacting the preachers' kids. A very long time passed before I finally could forgive just this one instance, and there were so many more.

But I want to give a glimpse of the issue with this scenario from the perspective of a preacher's kid. With all my heart and soul, I'm writing that this one incident is and was enough for me to turn away from the church. And here's exactly why.

I perceived that my dad was not being treated fairly by his superiors; those whom had hired him. Then the realization that he didn't even work for these jerks. They had not called my dad to pastor their church; God had. They had not given my dad instructions and guidelines; God had. They had not established his duties; God had.

Yet from the beginning, the deacons were in control. Or at least, they thought they were. I have worked in the secular world for almost thirty-five years now, and I have never been treated as poorly by my superiors as my dad was treated by a group of ignorant deacons for most of his almost sixty years of ministry.

Validation of the Family Altar

Not enough words can be written to express how important I believe the family altar is to a preacher's family or any family for that matter. As mentioned in other places of this book, my brothers and me all serve the Lord and I believe it is directly related to the family altar.

However, our family table suffered, and many times did not validate the family altar. Validation occurs only if the family table is an extension of the family altar. The same love, the same grace, the same mercy, the same concern, all these things and more must extend to the relationship between the preacher, his wife, and their kids.

In this context, both the family altar and the family table are literal. But they are both so much more a metaphor of the family unit in the parsonage than two literal places or occurrences. If the family table, meaning any time away from prayer and scripture study, in any way differentiates from the teachings of the scriptures, the scriptures then become void and meaningless to the kids.

As a preacher's kid, I often felt I lived in a make-believe world. I heard the praying, preaching, and teaching. Yet I saw very little to indicate any of it was reality. The infighting in the church stressed my dad so much that his children were scarred for the remainder of their lives as I'm sure is the story for thousands of preachers' kids.

I feel my teenage rage even as I write this book almost five decades later. Shut up! Shut up! I wanted to say shut up so many times. Leave us alone! Let my dad have some peace instead of driving him crazy with frivolous and meaningless issues. Of course, this must be one of the reasons most preachers move around an awful lot to the tune of about three or four years per church. But not my dad, he toughed it out. And he is not appreciated for any of his services.

Many congregants have come and gone over the years and now the church is small. Do you think any of these hundreds and hundreds ever come back to thank him? The answer is, *never!* I hate this. While I know Dad and Mom have always worked for God, it would have been nice for the people to show a little gratitude.

Our family table was broken. We could not have a normal meal. Something or someone seemed to always mess it up even on holidays. In 1984, I purchased my first video camera which then was called a camcorder. Thanksgiving was the first family gathering since my purchase. My brothers and me were all grown by now but still looked forward to being around Mom's table with her great home cooking. I set my camcorder on the tripod and started recording.

My intent was to record a memory of a happy time. And it was a happy time. Unbelievably, there were no interruptions. The phone didn't ring one time. There was no mention of church or church members. It was all about us. Mom had made everyone's favorite dish. Dad, always wanting to please, had spent a small fortune for all the food.

Recently, I pulled the old VHS from a file cabinet and viewed that special thanksgiving. I watched and listened through teary eyes. So much has happened since that happy Thanksgiving of 1984. We are no longer that same family. True, we get together about once a year, but it will never be that way again as it was in 1984. I'm glad I recorded the event against every else's wishes.

If that one special 1984 day had been reminiscent of the usual family table, I believe our family would be the same today. But sadly, that was an exception and not the norm. If that time were reminiscent of the normal table, the family altar would have been validated. But it was not.

Thousands, maybe millions, of preachers' kids have turned from the Gospel of Christ as an integral part of their lives. I'm suggesting a major cause is the lack of validation of the family altar. And the validation extends much farther than a table where food is consumed.

This is a cancer on Christianity in general. Church members do not live what they proclaim to be.

There was never hypocrisy in my childhood home in terms of my parents and their living the Gospel. The hypocrisy came in the disconnect between a happy home free of stress and a supposedly Christian home where all is okay. The true hypocrisy is that I lived in an extremely stressful environment where almost everything was deemed wrong, and no one seemed truly happy.

I remember my mom telling me long after I had left home of how Dad would come home on Sunday nights and sit up half the night in his recliner, depressed. Depressed? Over what? Simple answer, church members. Maybe, it was an ongoing conflict in the church (which there always was). Or maybe his sermon seemed to have fallen on deaf ears.

For many years, the worst night of the year was the annual business meeting of the church. Dad dreaded this meeting for months. I remember these meetings to be turbulent with the air filled with an evil spirit. I watched my dad remain calm and act as the peacemaker and at the same time saw church members full of devilish spirits argue and complain.

I even remember a preacher who attended the church placing a paper on the bulletin board in the vestibule for members to list complaints to meet the requirement to be heard in the meeting. To qualify, these issue/complaints had to be posted two weeks prior to the meeting.

What was this preacher thinking? Let's fight? Let's get our way? Don't sit back and let the deacons run the church without your input? I can't answer any of these questions, but here are mine. Why wouldn't you pray and seek God for his direction over all the issues for the meeting? Why would anyone be concerned about members siding together on issues?

The preacher who posted the list has gone on now, and I believe on to heaven. Because I believe the postings later became a regret. And I'm sure the preacher repented at some point. However, the preacher became engulfed in the carnality of the flesh. And the spirituality which would have led to an entirely different approach was totally absent. The result is the family altar, or all things spiritual not being validated by the enactment.

I understood why my dad hated these meetings. At some point, I made the decision to never attend another church business meeting, and for over three decades, I have not. And I will not ever subject myself to witnessing the devils come out in so-called Christians.

I understand from my mom that the business meetings have not been bad in recent years. While this may be true, I believe the only reason is that the membership is now small and very old. Too old to fight any more. But it never had to be the way it was.

Through my eyes, the entire church world was fake. Not necessarily that my parents failed, but everyone else did. I questioned why my parents would choose to take the heat. In fact, my dad left a good job with a grocery chain to become a full-time pastor. Why? I thought.

The pay was never good. The benefits were just okay but certainly didn't compare to what Dad could have obtained through the large grocery chain. And complaints were handled by a human resource team. Also, there was a union for filing grievances when the employee was treated unfairly.

Where does a pastor go when treated unfairly? He has no recourse. He cannot depend or utilize support from congregants. If he did accept support, the perception would be that he was in a clique. Additionally, he cannot be divisive. He must always be neutral at an attempt to keep peace in the church.

My mom and dad attempted to be as much like Christ as possible in an unintentional act to validate the family altar. They never realized the battle they were fighting. What good are scriptures if not applied? I was a preacher's kid who quickly knew the application was missing from most everyone but them.

While growing up, I never saw the family altar validated. I never saw the scriptures in terms of how a Christian should act, manifested. Fortunately, many years after my childhood, I finally began to see the validation. And thus, I began to value the family altar even in the shadows of the failure of the family table.

I know I'm not alone in both my experiences and perceptions. And I don't pretend to believe I have all the answers for preachers' kids or the preachers. But what I do know is history. I can view my past in living color clearer than any high definition I've ever seen. I see the lies and hypocrisy clearly. With equal clarity, I see the truth.

My story and perceptions cannot change the path for me or my brothers or any other preachers' kids. None of us can undo the tracks of our lives. We own them. We wear them. We are motivated by them. We are depressed by them. We are scarred by them. We are encouraged by them. We are strengthened by them. We are destroyed by them. All occurring simultaneously.

If I could speak to an unlimited audience of preachers with kids under the age of eleven, here is what I would say. Make sure there is a family altar. Make sure there is a family table. And most importantly, make sure the altar is validated. And I believe I know how. Good news, the mass exodus of preachers' kids from the Gospel can be stopped if the preacher's home is on red alert.

Build a Wall

There has been much talk in the last few years about building a wall on the borders of our country. The intent is to keep the illegal out. Regardless of one's opinion on an immigrant wall, building a wall around anything protects whatever is behind the wall. Over history, many walls have been built for protection. However, the walls made by man can succumb to damage and even to complete failure. They simply won't stand forever without maintenance.

On the other hand, a spiritual wall cannot fail. Preachers must build a spiritual wall around them and their children. The wall must be made of the right materials and must be created together. There are many examples of literal and spiritual walls that have been discussed. And one can research until content on the right discussion.

However, I'm going down my own path and suggesting my own type of wall. I'm suggesting a type of wall based on what I think would have been beneficial to me as a child and through my teenage years. I'm not going to use references. I'm using only my memory.

As I have attempted to write this book, I've been tempted to stop many times, more than I can say. And many times I did stop. I've been writing for over ten years off and on. The temptation to stop is my lack of confidence that anything I could possibly write could help preachers' kids, preachers, and congregants. Especially, at this juncture about building a wall.

But I'm resisting the temptation to stop even with no semblance of a publication on the horizon. If no one else ever reads this or receives any kind of help, I have been richly blessed with reflection and gratitude while writing my own thoughts without consultation from anyone except the Lord. So I'll proceed with my wall description and hope it helps stop the exodus and even possibly brings a preacher's kid or two back home again.

I believe the first ingredient in the wall is setting expectations. Innocently, my parents painted a picture of success of Christianity winning, of spiritual victory, of the costs of serving God outweighing the disadvantages, of the immense importance of making an eternal decision.

But what they could not paint was the reality or what I was to expect. They probably feared facing the ugly truth. The irony is the ugly truth sets the expectations. Because in the church, it gets mighty ugly. But I don't think my dad wanted to admit the ugliness even to himself much less his children.

However, the absence of acknowledgment does not minimize the impact on the preacher's kid. I experienced disappointment after disappointment in the church. I never felt safe in the church of vipers. Now, we didn't pass around rattlesnakes; we didn't need to. We had plenty of snakes sitting on the pews spewing their venom regularly.

What if my dad and mom had known to set the expectations? Would it have gone something like this? Maybe, they would have begun three-part family altar segments. The first part would be to read scripture, the second to pray, and the third discuss the reality.

Many times, Dad read from Matthew 7:13, "*Enter ye in at the strait gate: for wide is the gate, and broad is the way, that leadeth to destruction, and many there be which go in there at.*" He explained that "many" would go the wrong way in the world. But I believe I accepted this scripture as a separation of Christians and sinners as two general groups. The reality is it's more about the complete separation of people which includes all the church members.

I'm suggesting a preacher at his family altar to use this as a platform for expectations. Just taking the terms "straight gate" and "wide gate" in deeper explanation. For example, the preacher can explain to his kids that the gates cannot be used interchangeably. The straight gate is only for the Christians who have embodied the entire word of God as a lifestyle. The wide gate is for everyone else including practicing Christians in the church.

Preachers can honestly inform their kids to put this theory into place the next time they attend church by looking at the number of attendees—apply simple mathematics. How many of the congregants would be considered many? And how many of the congregants would be considered few?

Bottom line. The majority would be considered "many." This is setting clear expectations. Most people that attend church even faithfully are not going to enter the "straight" gate. I believe the perception for most preachers' kids early on is backward. I believed that most, if not all, church members were going to heaven and therefore, will act like it. What a miscalculation that was.

Then the miscalculation sets up extreme disappointment when the church members act out. Let me repeat myself here. The meanest people I've ever met attend church regularly. The preacher must set the stage for the kids. Tell them how mean church folks can be. And tell them why. They are not really Christians!

Explain to the kids that they will rarely encounter a true Christian as the gate is not wide. Therefore, expect to see bad things in the church. Expect those who praise aloud and say amen the loudest to be the biggest hypocrites. Expect most deacons to be self-consumed, power-hungry men who think they have been anointed to be disciplinarians, budget managers, church decision makers, and the pastor's boss.

Explain to the kids to expect most of the women members who do most of the work to be the biggest whiners and complainers because they do the work. Expect them to be jealous if anyone else receives credit for what they have done. Expect them to be offended if the preacher doesn't specifically ask for them to perform a task or plan an event.

Explain to the kids the rebuke they're going to be receiving just for being a preacher's kid. Tell them they will be ridiculed for every mistake. Tell them they will be held accountable at higher levels than any other kids by most people. And they will be expected to be perfect kids.

Set the expectations for worship, and that most will have no clue as to what worship even means. Explain that worship and

Christianity do not necessarily go hand in hand. Describe the reactions by the congregants to the preacher's sermons. Explain that the congregants will mostly not apply the sermons to their everyday lives.

Set the expectations for their own callings and/or talents and how they may not be accepted in the local church. My mom often offered the excuse that the Bible says a prophet has no honor in his hometown. She meant well but this doesn't apply here. The reason has nothing to do with hometown for preachers' kids. It's all about whether the congregants accept the preachers' kids or not.

My middle brother had a tremendous singing voice. He began singing at a very young age around five years old. When he was in high school, he was a featured soloist at concerts. I remember the Christmas concert in his senior year. He sang the beautiful Christmas song, "White Christmas." At the conclusion, he received a standing ovation. I was so proud! And honestly, I thought Bing Crosby had never sung it any better than my brother had that night.

Sadly, our congregation never appreciated his gift. He sang many times, and the older he grew, the less impact he had on the congregation. Others would sing, and the church would respond. When he sang, they sat on the pews with deadpan looks. I remember him saying to me concerning the congregation. "They don't care if I sing or not." And I think he was right. But why?

Simple. He was one of the preacher's sons. Maybe, it was jealously from the congregants. Maybe, they had hoped their child was the one singing. Maybe, they resented the opportunity my brother had been given. We'll never really know, but it does remind me of the congregant's children. My experience was that most church member's children were not Christians.

I remember looking around the congregation many times and seeing the parents and wondering what happened to their kids. True, some were grown and moved away. But most were just not attending church anywhere. So what went wrong there? The irony to me was that these same parents always seemed to know how I was supposed to act, who I was supposed to be, yet they had lost control of their own kids. And look where they were now. Some experts!

After setting expectations, the next part of the wall is acceptance. Preachers must learn to accept their kids for who they are and who they will become. Some may be talented while others are not. For example, my middle brother and I were always out in front. My youngest brother was and is quiet and stayed mostly in the background.

Who was most successful? Both. My youngest brother is a fine man who has successfully raised two fine young men. He has been married to his wife for over thirty years and is a real family man. My middle brother equally is a family man married over thirty years with two very successful daughters.

However, in most preachers' families, there is an expectation for leadership. This is an expectation that can be detrimental to a preacher's kid finding his or her place not only in the church but in society. Preachers cannot and should not try to force leadership on their kids.

Preachers need to learn to build a wall of acceptance around their kids. Assure them that it is okay if they don't preach, sing, teach, lead, or exhibit some specific talent. Love them through their inadequacies. Praise them for who they are, not what they have the potential to become.

Preachers need to apply this because no one else will. By nature, others will expect the preachers' kids to be talented leaders and to be like their parents. Anything that falls short of that is considered failure. Know for certain the preachers' kids will hear this along the way. "That kid is sure not like his dad."

When a preacher's kid hears this, it's not enlightening. No rockets burst in your head to remind you to be like your dad. Consequently, the adverse occurs. The kid will resent the comparison and do whatever it takes to widen the gap of comparison to his or her father or mother.

Preachers often make the mistake of trying to groom their kids into the ministry. Were they groomed into the ministry by their parents? If they are honest, they would say, no. At some point, they were called into the ministry. Here lies the mystery of why preachers consciously or unconsciously try to extend their call to their kids.

When I was born, my parents were best friends with another couple who lived in a duplex next to them. Both men were preachers who became pastors. Subsequently, they began their families. My parents had three boys, and the other pastor and his wife had three girls.

I don't know how old I was when I first heard them make a proclamation amongst themselves. My dad would say, "We'll raise the preachers, and you guys raise the preachers' wives." They would laugh and agree together. Of course, I know they were saying this in jest to some degree. They knew they couldn't be absolute in this plan. But at the same time, they were hoping. Both that we would marry each other, and that we would be preachers and preachers' wives. This was the beginning of my thinking that the expectation was for me to be a preacher.

Let's compare to secular careers. For example, if a politician's child is not a politician, they are not considered a failure. Same for lawyers, doctors, pilots, or any career. It may be true that the parents desire their offspring to follow in their footsteps, but if they try to force the path, the opposite usually occurs.

But here's the major difference. If a doctor's child chooses to work for the railroad or become a plumber or electrician, no real harm is done. But a preacher's kid who does not become a preacher usually does not become a Christian. The difference is eternal. The ramifications are for an extremely unhappy life here and even worse in the next life.

I believe the career choice is directly related to the level of acceptance the preacher's kid received in the parsonage. Was it okay that I would not become a preacher? Probably. But as far as I was concerned, there was no option. My battle was that I wanted to be a pastor, puzzling.

But what if a preacher's kid wanted to do something entirely different? He or she must be assured, that God can use someone in every occupation in the world. And we need Christians in every field.

Acceptance in the parsonage is also allowing the kids to be themselves and not carbon footprints of someone's perception of what a preacher's kid should be. This is not a free pass to become a loudmouth activist against anything and everything in the church. Quite the contrary, acceptance of individual personalities allows creativity within the preachers' kids.

The parsonage should be a refuge as any home should be. A place where expression with respect for others is encouraged. A place where it is permissible to ask why? As a preacher's kid, I wanted to ask why many times. Why were the people angry? Why did I have to be concerned with the opinions of every church member. Why does the word of any church member supersede my own words?

I'm eternally grateful that my dad was a strict disciplinarian. He taught me respect, duty, responsibility, accountability, and trust. What I struggled with was the discipline when it was directly related to who I was. I expected to receive the rod of punishment if I lied. But because I lied, not because I was a preacher's son who lied.

During my teen years, my parents went out of town to a church conference somewhere, and I stayed in a church member's home. I don't remember the specifics, but I remember I skipped school to hang out with a girl a little older and who had a car. Other than the skipping classes, it was innocent. We went to the local mall and ate a baked pretzel. I felt guilty because I was doing something wrong; however, I was a normal kid who simply gave in to temptation.

I didn't expect to get caught, but if I did, I did expect to be punished. I have no recollection of how I was found out, but I was. The two things I remember about this event were what was said to me by the church member with whom I was staying, and the first words of my dad when he spoke to me.

The church member was nice. I'll give her that. But here is what she said that cut me deeply. "Frankie," she said, "I would have expected skipping from any other kid but not the preacher's kid." Let's stop here and evaluate what she said. Any kid may be expected to skip school on any given occasion. However, a preacher's kid should never be expected to skip school.

Her response made no sense to me then. And five decades later, it still makes no sense. A kid is a kid. What is the difference? A policemen's kid, a preacher's kid, a plumber's kid, a teacher's kid, a president's kid, an electrician's kid, a utility worker's kid. They're all the same. They are just kids with the same propensity to make bad decisions.

Then came the words from my dad. He said, "Son, do you have any idea how embarrassing this is for me what you have done?" There it is. The direct correlation to who I was to what I had done. Bottom line is I was wrong no matter whose kid I was. And I deserved to be punished, which I was.

This scenario seemed to repeat itself over and over in my youth. With each occasion, I resented more each time with the reminder that I was a preacher's kid and should be different. My dad innocently without malice continued down the only path he knew. I assume it made sense to him that the reminder of my title would breed sorrow, repentance, and correction. However, resentment was the only emotion I bore from the lessons.

A wall of acceptance absents itself from the title, preacher's kid. The wall of acceptance is not a premise for condoning acts that are wrong. It places emphasis on the wrong doings. Acceptance doesn't care who you are; it loves through repentance, discipline, and correction. Acceptance is loving the child enough to correct the mistake with an explanation of the wrong followed by discipline and correction without any mention of the father's occupation.

No one would ever debate which murder committed was worse. The one by the preacher's kid or the one by the painter's kid. So why should pastors and their wives place any emphasis at all on their own occupation as it relates to the actions of their kids? I am one of thousands and thousands of living examples that prove it doesn't work.

The next part of the wall that should be built in the parsonage by the parents is support. Like acceptance, support can be confused with condoning. To be clear, support does not include condoning any wrong. In fact, in this context, support has nothing to do with right or wrong. Support is the ability to provide backing.

Alert to all pastors: If your kid is right, support them even against the membership. These are your flesh and blood. They will always be family. The church members will come and go, mostly go. Don't worry about your own wellbeing. Don't you believe God will stand for you when you stand for your kids?

I firmly believe the calling to the ministry should always come first, and I am not compromising or conflicting this belief by telling pastors to support their kids. You can put the ministry first and still support your kids. Members will ultimately respect you for your parental support if the support is rendered and described in a Christlike manner.

The church members probably won't agree. But the long-term benefit is the kids will appreciate the support and see the connection to the ministry. After all, Christ supported kids and even scolded his disciples for pushing them away.

The challenge for pastors is the fear of showing partiality or favoritism to their kids. Let's think about this for a moment. Shouldn't all parents favor their own kids? Shouldn't all parents be partial to their own kids? If so, then why is it wrong for preachers to do so? The members certainly favor their kids unabashedly. And it's just the natural parental instinct. So preachers act natural to your kids.

If members react negatively, preachers should use their communication skills to bring into perspective the love and support for one's kids. Of course, this assumes they have good communication skills. I've found these skills aren't necessarily inherent to preachers even though they are public speakers.

In the end, if the members don't understand, side with your kid. The long-term implications far outweigh the short-term gain you may achieve with the church member. Trust me, church members are not loyal to pastors. This becomes evident the first time the preacher displeases the member. Then all loyalty goes out the window. So why not support your kid? The members will be discontent for many other reasons and may eventually leave. But you still have your kid.

I respect my dad for always being the peacemaker. But I wish he could have known how much his support would have meant to us boys. He did so many things right and most of all, loved us. He set the right example. He provided for us, and we never went without. He taught us how to go to heaven and live for Jesus. But innocently, he let the church members have the advantage over us.

I'm not suggesting that my dad or any pastor should fight with the members over the kids. Support does not have to mean fighting.

Support does not have to mean division. Support just means backing your own kids when they are right. I'm suggesting all pastors with children take heed to this idea of a support wall.

Church members are like predators. They take advantage of the lesser. If they see an inroad where the pastor is not building a wall around his kids, they will swoop in for the kill. The attack will then be relentless. At every turn, the preacher's kid will face opposition. And most importantly, the members will make sure everybody knows every mistake the preachers' kids make.

To be sure, all church members are not vicious preacher's kid's killers. A minority of members are relatively supportive. Although it pains me to give any credit to church members, many members have no clue as to the damage they have done and are doing to the preachers' kids. Good news, I can help.

Church Members and the Preachers' Kids

I have been extremely hard on church members regarding my youth and with good cause. Church members made my life very difficult growing up. I thought church members were mean and sometimes ruthless with every intent to make my life miserable. Many years would pass before I could both forgive them and try to understand them. Over these years, I've made many observations. None of which could be proven in court, but all of which are real to me.

The first observation is that the church members treated me the way they did out of envy. They witnessed firsthand the way we were being raised. They acknowledged we were living in a spiritual realm all the time. And when the church doors were opened, we were there. And I believe they noticed we didn't seem to mind the world in which we lived.

Therefore, they envied what they observed and wished the same for their kids. Interestedly, they could have provided the same environment for their kids but did not. I can honestly say without reservation that I never stayed in a member's home where a family altar was in place. And I stayed many nights in many homes over my childhood years.

Not one time was there a mention of prayer or Bible reading before bedtime, not one time. Let's start here. How would they expect their kids to have the same Bible knowledge that I had? They never read the scriptures to their kids, and I was read to every single night. They never taught their kids to pray. Our dad taught us and required us to pray every night.

I would suggest church members install the family altar in their own homes instead of expecting the pastors and Sunday school teachers to do all the teaching to their kids. They would look at me like a nasty bug because they had failed to instill the faith in their own kids. But it was at their fingertips. They failed their own kids and took it out on me. And I believe this is and was repeated across the world.

I believe the second issue with church members and preachers' kids is the same as with the preachers and their wives which I mentioned earlier. Setting expectations too high. The church members expect preachers' kids to set the example for their own kids.

This one I've never completely had a grasp on. What would possibly make a church member think this way? No one should ever put this kind of pressure on a kid. They're just a kid! Why should a preacher's kid set the example? Because he or she is a preacher's kid? What difference does that make?

Let's apply this principle globally. Should an algebra teacher's child set the example in the class for the highest math skills? Should the music teacher have the most gifted child in music? Should the polished public speaker's child be the greatest orator? Should the plumber's kid be the best pipefitter? I could go on, but you get the drift.

If I had an audience with church members who attend a church where the pastor has young kids, I would employ them to not set expectations any higher for the preachers' kids than for their own kids. Remember, they're just regular kids. They just happen to have a pastor for a father.

I would tell church members to love the pastor's kids, show them support, and understand they are already under the microscope. A single church member can be the difference in the life of a preacher's kid. I would have given anything for a church member to have taken me under their wing. I would have loved a confidant other than my parents; someone I could have gone too. And someone that could have helped me communicate to my own parents. I had no one.

I know it is not the responsibility of the church member to spiritually adopt the preacher's kid. But if one had spiritually adopted me and helped me through the difficult times, what a huge difference it would have made. And what about all the preachers' kids who have left the church and the Gospel? Maybe, a church member could have made the difference between staying or departing.

What a dynamic and impactful ministry of a church member to the preachers' kids! For most of my life, I've viewed the church members as my enemies, and it was true most of the time. But it did not have to be that way. I can't go back though I wish I could. But if you're a church member, you can make a difference in a young preacher's kid in your church. Don't miss a life altering opportunity.

But the most important thing a church member can do is be real. Church members can so easily turn non-Christians away permanently. And it's not just the preachers' kids. Someone who proclaims to be a Christian yet does not act the part will do more damage than any atheists could ever do.

My experiences which molded my thoughts about Christianity early in my life were with Christians. When one is a Christian and believes Jesus is the Christ, it is rare for that same person to be influenced away from that belief by a non-believer. The exception may be teenagers who are so impressionable.

Therefore, it is critical for adult Christians to be steadfast and consistent in their walk with the Lord. Someone is always watching. And in church, that someone is a teenager. I remember being a teenager and knowing the difference between what is real and not real. However, church people were confusing me. I just could not swallow watching someone praise in some demonstrative way or sing as if the Lord was all that mattered only to see that same person act like the devil.

On more than one occasion, I witnessed arguments after a church service. Now, I can understand arguments after a ball game or at a bar. Maybe, arguments are natural after supper or before bedtime. Normal may be to argue after a movie or a political debate. Certainly, many arguments occur on the job. But at church? After service? After the Word of God has been espoused? After praise and worship? How could this be?

I'll tell you how this happens. Because adult Christians have not accepted their responsibility to emulate the Lord. At that moment, it's all about them. They don't stop to think who is watching and listening. The kids are taking it all in, and these arguments are making lifetime impacts. The adult Christians don't have a clue. Then wonder why their kids stray away from the church and the Lord.

The missing ingredient in almost every Christian home is consistency. When there is no consistency in the home, there will be no consistency in the church. I've never detected a sense of urgency or accountability among church members. Consistency? A joke!

The typical church member attends church to be either entertained or fulfilled. I know this because neither rarely occurs in a true Gospel church. Hence, grumbling and complaining enters. The mission of the church is not to entertain. The mission of the church is to evangelize. The church service should be a time for refueling to accomplish the mission.

The preacher's kid knows the mission of the church inherently. Unfortunately, this knowledge backfires. I have seen so many church members who had no clue as to the mission of the church other than some selfish desire to be the center of attention. As a preacher's kid, the reality of the mission dims like a flashlight with a dying battery, slow but sure; church member by church member.

I don't presume to speak for all preachers' kids, but I'm guessing it's the same on a universal level. The reality of Christianity and all it should be and contain is missed inside the church walls. I was never surprised or disappointed by non-Christians. I didn't expect any type of standard. But I did expect church members to be something different.

For example, would anyone ever expect cruelty to be exhibited in a church? I saw cruelty many times. I remember one choir director conducting auditions for members. Now, on some level, I understand choir members need to be able to sing. But on the other hand, a willing heart who wants to sing for the Lord should not be denied.

But it wasn't just the denial, it was the cruel way the persons were told. First, they were humiliated with an audition then told they could not be a member of the choir. Totally forgotten was the mission. To my knowledge, those persons who were rejected are no longer in church anywhere.

So what was accomplished? The best singers were in the choir? Score one for the choir director. He won. But at what costs? Souls were turned away. Souls felt no worth, yet with God, they were invaluable. But what they felt was rejection. And worse, it is highly unlikely they will ever find their way back to church.

The next most demonstrative anti-Christian tactics church members employ is the formation of cliques. The non-inclusive clubs create divisions and ratify separatism and exceptionalism. I understand the natural tendency to migrate to those most like ourselves. But the damage to those outside who are not accepted in the group can be catastrophic in terms of soul damage.

These cliques are not ambiguous and are illuminated like neon signs of advertisement. In every church, everyone can identify the cliques. But how do they form? I believe these cliques form innocently enough. In the defense of the clique members, I don't think they start with an intention to form an exclusive club.

So how does it happen? The genesis is on the social platform. Invites to social gatherings as simple as going out to lunch after church can be the beginning of segregation in the church. Sadly, cliques promote segregation. And worse, this segregation is not based on race, creed, or color. It's the segregation of the children of God, the Bride of Christ.

Notice I use the terms cliques and segregation interchangeably. Because there is no difference between the two. Neither have a place in the body of Christ. If we look to the perfect model Jesus himself, we would not find any instance of him segregating himself from others. Yet church members justify this behavior in every church I've attended.

But why? Because as Christians, no different than non-believers, we struggle with associating with those who are different from us. Maybe, the difference is personality. Or it could be the clothes others wear. Another culprit, the background of others tends to lead us to separation.

The list of reasons for segregation in the church is infinite. The reasons are also inexcusable. The church is the very last place any hint of segregation should exist. How can a body of believers come together in worship and expect God to dwell among them when there are divisions in the sanctuary?

If we can't join united with all believers in the church, where can we? The answer is not heaven. Psalms 133:1 says, "Behold, how good and how pleasant it is for brethren to dwell together in unity." Heaven will be unified. If we can't be unified here, we will never see that land of indescribable beauty.

More emphatically, the Bible tells us in Proverbs 6:16–19 that there are seven things God hates and guess what number seven is? He hates one who sows discord among the brethren. Wow! In other words, he hates segregation of his son's body.

When a church member acts in a non-inclusive manner with other believers regardless of their differences, the church member becomes an enemy of God. To all church members who are currently doing this, God hates you! Harsh? You better believe it's harsh. So discontinue your cliques.

As a preacher's kid, I saw both sides of the segregation in the church. Sometimes, I was invited in the "popular" group, and sometimes, I wasn't. I remember feeling bad when I was asked to go out after church when I knew certain others were not included.

I'm embarrassed to admit that at times, the segregation rubbed off on me. I too created and participated in cliques. Many times, my wife and I had small circle of friends. Ironically, these friends were usually not good for me, and I fell under the wrong influence. These experiences allow me to retroactively see the devastation of segregation.

I have learned the larger the circle, the lesser the influence of a few within the circle. Also, the larger the circle, the stronger the individual. When the circle is larger and more inclusive, the pressure to "fit" in is minimized or even eliminated, just makes sense. In a large group where all individuals are important, no one is singled out.

In a larger sense, segregation not only conflicts with the body of Christ but defies the body of Christ. If we are all parts of the body of Christ, how can we segregate the parts? Would we segregate our own body? We would not ignore our right hand because it has an ugly scar.

We would not disassociate with our right ear and refuse to use it for listening because the lobe is too long. How silly. But when we treat other believers who are a part of the body of Christ unfairly or unequally, we're segregating our own body parts one from another.

To understand the magnitude of segregation in the church, one must only look at the racial divide. Before any other division, the church must recognize race as the most prevalent. Why is it that whites and blacks cannot worship together? And who decided? Why are there all-white churches and all-black churches?

All white and all black are not the problem. If so, it would mean the color of a man's skin is significant as it relates to the worship of God. Is it the music? No. White churches are diverse in music and black churches are diverse in music. Is it the structure of the services? No. Every white church is different from each other. Same for black churches. So what is it? It's simple. The division is just another division Satan inspired. He will do anything to break apart the Body of Christ.

The church should be free from all prejudice and divisions. I'm suggesting the complete lack of Christianity in any church who has proverbial walls up to divide for any reason. Whether it's race, personality, grievances, social status, or conceit, none of these have any place in the house of God.

Speaking as a preacher's kid, I was appalled at the various levels of prejudice in the church. The first level, I call the spiritual boom. These are the so-called Christians who believe God has set the divisions. Apparently, they have been lifted on a boom far above others where they have heard from God concerning this matter.

They repeat such ludicrous words such as, "God doesn't intend from us to be together. He made them different. They need to have their own place to worship." I am curious if these spiritual boomers think heaven is segregated; maybe, a heavenly Chinatown, a heavenly Motown, a heavenly white area.

The second level, I call the trampoline brigade. They jump from one view to the other. If among their own kind, they're prejudice. But when someone different is in the midst, they jump over to brotherhood. Who do they believe they are fooling? Certainly not God.

The third level I call, the silent marchers. These are the quiet folks who don't say much in crowds and are never out front. But they are extremely effective in blocking progress in the church by consistently gathering in voting blocks. They are usually good tithe payers and are long time members. They stand against any "change" which includes embracing those who are different.

Today, nothing in the churches has changed except tactics. The looming question for any local church is how to grow the numbers of attendees. The funny thing is the tactics are all wrong. The aforementioned problems in the church that are the true detriments for attracting new comers are still not addressed.

Rather, the music has now changed to a more conducive ambiance to draw a younger crowd. The preaching has been modified to appeal to a broader spectrum of congregants. And more radically, program after program has been added to address every possible "segregated" group. Odd how people of all ages and backgrounds used to gather in the same sanctuary.

I'm told the appeal must change for a church to be successful. This means larger numbers of people attending. But are they not covering up and burying the real issues as if they don't exist? What if people are more entertained than ever? In terms of numbers, this methodology works. If you liberalize, they will come.

How are the changes affecting church members? Are they developing spiritually? Are they more like Christ than ever before? Are their testimonies more powerful? Are miracles of deliverance from Satan's power occurring? From my perspective, the answer is no to all the above.

If not these, then what are the results? I'm suggesting comfort for all. Everyone feels good about themselves. Segregation is justified. After all, segregation is a natural phenomenon when ten thousand folks attend the same church. It's impossible not to have cliques.

Therefore, it is justified, and everyone is comfortable in their own "small group."

Does this mean large churches are not spiritual? No. However, people get lost in the large numbers and the problems so illuminated in a small church appear to be non-existent in the large ones. But far worse issues exist. The lukewarm syndrome is alive and well. Sadly, they don't even know they're lukewarm because the "feel good" sermons allow them to lead happy lives without conviction.

Give yourself a pat on the back if you're a pastor or member in one of these churches. You've done it! The pews are filled, and money is coming in for more programs and more buildings. You can now erect buildings for everyone one for the divorced, one for the youth, one for the singles, one for the old, one for the addicts, one for the new converts, one for the newlyweds, and maybe, one for the disenfranchised.

But don't stop there, build another one for the super Christians, the role models. These are the super staffers who are paid handsome salaries for their innovative segregated ideas and programs. Everyone is excited, and growth is unlimited. Someone say halleluiah! Oops, we don't say that anymore, do we? Sorry.

Now, give yourself a kick in the rear. You completely missed the mission of the church. You foolishly have overlooked kingdom building which is what the disciples set out to do. You're establishing community centers where participants are made to feel good not holy places of worship where sinful souls are convicted of their sins.

The member is being fed, no doubt. But what are they eating? Certainly not the meat of the word. And here's why. Meat chewing takes strong teeth and strong jaws. The modern-day church member has neither. Pastors are feeding the members as if they are infants, so they can gum their food. For God's sake, don't give them anything that is tough to chew or that will make them choke. If you do they'll leave.

To address the real problem in the church which is lack of spiritual commitment and dedication, truth must be expounded. We must tell the truth. Non-church members are not looking for what they already have. They want something real. Something that is different and will make them different.

So here lies the dilemma for preachers' kids. And not just preachers' kids but any kid that has been raised in a church. What do we do with what we have experienced? Ultimately, we must decide whether to serve Christ. Thousands upon thousands of church-reared kids end up deciding not to serve him. But why? The answer is the people in the church dim the light that once shined so brightly.

The Illumination of the Cross and the Way Back Home

According to the Bible, two men walked on water, Jesus and Peter. We often forget that Peter walked because he also fell and nearly drowned, typical of many of us. We follow Christ for a while until we are distracted. Consequently, we fall and begin to sink. This following and falling is questioned in the Bible.

Galatians 5:7 asks, "Ye did run well; who did hinder you that ye should not obey the truth?" Notice the question is who, not what. Interestingly, people are the conduit Satan uses to infiltrate our souls to the point of disillusion. Thus, people cause other people to fall. People are the distraction.

In Peter's fall, it was the angry waves and the howling swift winds pushing against what he was accomplishing that distracted him from Jesus. We can humanize the angry waves and howling winds. The angry waves in the church are the critical voices we hear. The howling blowing winds are the ones who disappoint us with their hypocrisy and spiritual deceit causing us to doubt.

What would have happened to Peter if he had not allowed distraction? Clearly, he would have continued walking on the water out to Jesus. The reality is the winds and waves did not prohibit Peter in any way from a successful walk on the water. They had no power over him until he gave them the power.

Retrospectively, I allowed the same power exchange. I gave my opposers the power to distract me. I could have made another choice. I could have stayed focused on the one who had called me in the first place. Just like Peter whom Jesus called, I could have walked with him. No one had the power to pull me off the track unless I allowed the power exchange. Sadly, like many other preachers' kids, I empowered those who were intentionally or unintentionally trying to destroy me.

How many times have I remembered the old evangelists who warned me that Satan would sift me like wheat? More than I can recall. I just didn't realize at the time that Satan was powerless unless I gave him the power to sift me. And I was oblivious to the ones he would use to do the sifting.

We will never know how the account of Peter walking on the water to meet Jesus would have been written had he not been distracted. I will never know what great things I could have accomplished for God had I not allowed distractions. I have relived my failures many times through shaded memories but have identified every intimate detail of the genesis of every distraction.

But I find no comfort in knowing the casual effects. I find no peace in understanding the church members and deacons. There is no consolation prize for me for hindsight which cannot be corrected resulting in indescribable emptiness. And this emptiness grew until I found the answer to the past, present, and future.

Like with Peter, Jesus is calling to us today to step out and come to him. Unlike Peter, we can't see him in the distance. We can't make out an image of a loving savior calling us to service. We can't see his smiling face and the compassion in his eyes. We can't hear his audible voice calling us over the turmoil all around us.

We can't trust and walk a few steps toward him with aspirations to touch his awaiting hands, at least, not yet. But we are not left hopeless to be battered and torn by the angry waves and winds. We need only to remember his final words from the cross, "It is finished."

What did he mean by this short statement? I believe the statement is open-ended. Whatever I need or will ever need is finished—complete. At that moment, my destiny was defined not as a reality but as a possibility when he uttered those victorious words. No guarantee as a reality because the responsibility to apply the completed work for my life is all on me. However, my possible divine destiny will only come to fruition based on my ability to believe and apply his words.

The concept of belief and application of his completed work for me is not profound. But is it difficult? Absolutely. He paid a great price to complete the work for me, and there is a price that I must pay as well. My price to pay is to eliminate all distractions from my life. This is my battle, my war. And I've struggled to stay in the battle.

What I have found after many distractions have hindered my service to him is there is a way that works. Something that will cause everything and everyone to fade in the distance. Something that will keep me focused on the goal. Something that will never fail me. Something that will keep my enemies at bay. Something that will turn my doubt into belief, my bitterness into love and joy, my resentment into fulfillment. It's the cross upon which he finished the task.

The cross must be our focal point as we navigate this worldly journey. The cross must become brightly lit in our memory though we were not there to see his great sacrifice so that we always know the way home. The illumination of the Cross will always lead us home, to him.

Our imagination must be vivid and sharp every single day. We can never take our eyes off the cross. If so, we will sink just like Peter. The account of his crucifixion must be read often. Meditating on his suffering will affect our vision and our hearing. We will see people in the light of his love from the cross. Our hearing will be deafened to the sounds of the world.

According to the Bible, a star led to the baby Christ. The cross replaces the star and leads everyone to the risen savior if we will follow. The cross must be viewed through repentant eyes of faith.

The cross alone is not magic, and the symbol has no powers. Wearing a cross as a necklace or hanging a replica on the wall will bring no power nor will it deliver us from evil. Only through a spiritual prism can one find the answer to life from the cross. What he did for me, just me, creates an overwhelming emotion within me that promotes service. No other depiction has such human emotion.

As a preacher's kid, I was introduced to the work on the cross as early as I can remember. But for most of my life, I let the cross abide in the background of my life as it played out, not purposely. I just never related distractions to the vision of the cross.

The terrifying question for me is how many days passed where I didn't think of the cross, not even once during the day. But I'm not alone, am I? As you are reading this, do you remember the last time you thought about the entire work on the cross and the suffering beyond imagination that was experienced by an innocent Son of God.

I believe it is completely impossible to view the reality of the suffering on the cross and not be moved to dedication. I remember reading about one of the observers that was there and experienced the gruesome death of our Lord. He said, "Truly this man was the Son of God."

I believe this is always the reaction to the cross. Otherwise, how can it be explained? Who could love to this degree? Who would allow such abuse? And for an innocent man? And for those who did not deserve such a gift. I look at the cross and find complete humility. How could he have done this for me?

How could I have failed him so many times? Looking at the cross, I cannot fail this savior who gave his all for me. But I did fail him and often. That's it! I failed him when I wasn't looking at the cross. Therefore, I can't fail him if I'm viewing him upon that cruel cross. I have no other desire except to please and serve him as long I see him suffering.

When I stand at the foot of the cross and look up at him, I lose all senses of who is around me and what they are saying. I can't hear their words of discouragement. I can't hear their criticisms. I can't hear the mocking. The sound is just a dull tone of a background noise of which I'm oblivious.

I don't' care who is around me, hypocrites or saints. I am not concerned about what the ones around me think about me. I don't care if I'm loved or hated, accepted or rejected, popular or unpopular, rich or poor, talented or untalented.

When I'm looking up at the cross and him who loved me so, no one can pull me away. No sin can distract me. Nothing the world can offer can even penetrate my thoughts for any consideration. I'm completely captivated by the one who is suffering such agony and the reason for his suffering.

The illumination of the cross upon which I gaze is so bright to the point of intoxication. I'm totally blinded by the light. I only see him who hangs there. I feel no fear. And the tempter is helpless in his efforts to distract me. He presses hard and tries to show me other scenes, but I only see the cross.

He assaults my body and my mind and inflicts pain. But I stand strong in the power of the illuminated cross. My pain is nothing to be compared to the one whom I view. I am molested yet not destroyed. I am attacked but not defeated. I am sifted like wheat but will not crumble.

Heaven is opened before me, and I can see the price being paid for my salvation. Simultaneously, I'm no longer selfish; I want everyone to see what I'm seeing and feel what I am feeling. Burst of praises come from my inner soul. I have no problems, no concerns. The only request I have is how can I serve.

Then reality hits. I can't stay at the foot of the cross. Or can I? Since it's not a physical presence, the possibilities are endless. But I have no choice if I want to eliminate distractions. Like Peter, I will surely begin to sink and ultimately, drown. I must find a way to continually view the illuminated cross.

Now comes the price I must pay. Just as a security system protects from burglaries, I need to invest in a detraction elimination system or DES. The DES is the cross but how do I keep it illuminated. It will be expensive; I'm certain. A light burning around the clock has an associated cost, and it won't be cheap.

Now that I've identified a credible DES, I must figure out how I can afford it. To me, the obvious culprit of falling away from Christ is distractions. Simply put, one cannot fall away unless they are distracted. And the Bible says it's human distractions as per the question aforementioned that ask who not what.

Due to the nature of what I have written regarding life as a preacher's kid, I believe it safe to say, while not exclusively, all preachers' kids need a DES. Every example of failure in my life relates to being distracted from what I was taught. As the Bible promised, I could not leave the teachings completely. But that did not mean, I would keep these on the forefront of my thinking.

The most comforting message I have felt from the cross is I can always come home. Though the light may have gone out either partially or completely, that same light can come back on and be brighter than ever. But I must account for the cost.

So what is the extreme cost of having the cross illuminated in my life daily? First, my life must change from that of self-indulgence to that of sacrifice. I must crucify my own desires and bury my personal goals. Everything I've ever wanted to accomplish must be erased from my heart as if they never had merit. Which they had no merit because they were based on my will not his.

Second, I must give up me. This strikes fear in many and goes against everything a psychologist or psychiatrist would say. Even Shakespeare mistakenly said, "To thine own self be true." To trust in the provision or intellect of any man, including ourselves, is a colossal miscalculation of judgment.

I cannot depend on me; I'm completely unreliable. And why would I rely on weakness instead of strength? Based on my track record, any reliance on myself would be foolish at best. I must become him. I must take on the persona of Jesus Christ. I must think like he thinks; feel like he feels; react and respond like he does; love like only he can; forgive beyond limitations as only he will.

A miscalculation of my own frailty is to doom any chance of eliminating distractions. I am my own most powerful and influential distraction because I am in control of myself. Yet I have no qualifications and am incapable of navigating external distractions while the internal distractions go unnoticed.

Third, I must give up my most precious possession, time. Ironically, I own no time. I deceive myself with a false sense of ownership. I cannot depend on one more breath. I have no idea when my life will end. So how can I take ownership of something to which I have no control?

I can't take ownership, but I can demonstrate an abandonment of foolish thinking and false pretenses. It's a minute-by-minute proposition. Therefore, I can only give one minute at a time; I have no promise of the next one.

Giving what I don't own, my time, is only possible in the short term. Therefore, every minute must count. My favorite television show must subside to Bible reading. My favorite activity or leisure minutes must be given over to times of prayer and communication with Jesus. My bodily weariness must be overshadowed by my faithfulness to the house of God where I must worship him in his sanctuary.

Now I'm getting the feel of the cost of keeping the cross illuminated before me. The apostle Paul said, "For me to live is Christ." I get it. I believe Paul is saying there is no other purpose to life but to follow Christ. It's a sacrifice. We are required to take up our own cross to follow him.

The cross we bear is rugged just as his was. It is full of suffering and laden with pain. How else can we identify with him? Not through extravagant lifestyles. Not through worldly success. Not through fame and fortune. These are not conducive to a life of service and will distract.

Of course, who wants to sacrifice? It was even hard for Christ. The nature of the man he became compelled him to ask that the cup be passed from him. Yet his higher compulsion was to do the will of the one who sent him. I must breed within myself the same passion for his will over my own. And I must feed the passion through the illumination of the cross.

The challenge is my own responsibility to keep the cross illuminated before me. I can't delegate to someone else. I can't even ask for prayer for assistance with this critical task. For the cross to work as a DES, I must stay focused. I can only do this by never taking a break from the focal point.

Keeping the cross illuminated is only possible through an intimate relationship with the one who hang on it. To be reminded of his sacrifice and to keep it on the forefront, I need consistent communication. Of course, this can only be accomplished through a dedicated prayer life. I must talk to him as much as humanly possible.

Through all my failings, the one consistent thing I can identify in every case was the absence of communication with Jesus. I never stopped praying, but the prayers were no more than blanket request prayers. Such as, Lord be with us, protect us, and please meet our needs. Occasionally, I would pray for someone else.

The total time spent praying was less than ten minutes on any given day. No wonder I failed him. No wonder I was distracted. No wonder I let people get to me and discourage me even turn me off. I had minimal communication with Jesus and therefore had no power. Worst, I gave very little thought to the cross.

As a preacher's kid, I relied on my teaching, and it served me well many times. But it wasn't a DES. Even when I was in the ministry, I did not pay the price to keep the cross illuminated and therefore, succumbed to external forces.

There is no big secret to survival as a Christian. The foundation of Christianity is Jesus, his birth, his life, his death, and his resurrection. The synergy begins and ends with his work on the cross. The only hope for mankind is the redemptive sacrifice Jesus made on the cross.

Consequently, many have a onetime experience with the cross. And that's not enough to sustain for any length of time. It's not a "visit" to the cross that's important. One must relocate to the cross—move in. The cross must be home base for all Christians. Imagine the church world if everyone proclaimed Christian's home base was the cross.

Forgiveness would be rampant. Because forgiveness is what exudes from the cross. Remember the words of Jesus from the cross when he said, "Forgive them for they know not what they do."

Sacrificing for others would be the mantra for Christians since the greatest sacrifice of all time comes from the cross. We would not be concerned about just ourselves and our families. We would love those who we know and who we've not yet met. Because the love from the cross is for all and is unconditional.

Imagine the boldness we can obtain from the cross to stand against Satan. After all, Jesus defeated the devil, death, and hell forever on the cross. We are empowered at the cross when we find victory is ours eternally. Eternal life and the hope of heaven is realized on the cross because Jesus won. He finished the fight for us!

There is power in the allurement of the cross. With the power comes fortification of the soul. With the fortification comes establishment. With establishment comes loyalty. However, none of these leave the outer perimeter of the cross. These are attached to the cross in such a manner that cannot be taken away as if a magnetic force was pulling like gravity our hearts and minds.

The question is, how big is the perimeter? It's important to understand the size as to keep the proper closeness to maintain the illumination. Just outside the perimeter, the cross fades. Then a little further and the cross disappears. Once the cross disappears, everything changes.

All things gained from the closeness to the cross are now lost. When this occurs, one is suspect to be overtaken by distractions. The sounds of divisive voices now become audible. Critical arrows aimed at the distant Christian now hits the target. Soon, the distance expands between the cross and the individual almost to the point of no return—almost.

The perimeter size is different for every individual. The distance is measured from the heart of the individual to the heart of the one on the cross. But how far is that? The distance is solely dependent upon individual's desire and willingness. I believe this is the true definition of taking up one's cross to follow him.

I'm no longer a young outspoken preacher's kid trying to make his own way. I'm no longer fighting church members. I'm no longer seeking the center of attention. But keeping myself within the perimeter of the cross is more important to me than ever even though I'm beginning my sixties.

After failures, stupidity, stubbornness, and pride, I've found the place I needed to be all along—at the foot of the cross. I should have never left for one minute, and I know that now. I should have made my proverbial home right there. My decisions would have been very different. My actions and reactions would have been very different. I would not have been so easily distracted. My entire life would have played out so that I would have been in the perfect will of God.

I may have been approaching retirement as a pastor at who knows where. I'm certain I would have never divorced. I would have taken the words of the loud evangelists seriously and would have not been sifted many times by the devil. I would have driven many miles down very different paths than the ones on which I was derailed.

My story could have been so different. And I believe many other preachers' kids have similar if not parallel stories. In different places, in different churches, with different parents, with different distractions, the one thing we have in common is we were pawns of Satan to stop the cycle.

I realize not all preachers' kids have chosen to leave their teachings, but many have. I'm blessed in that I found the answer at the cross before it was too late, and now I have good news for every other preacher's kid who has strayed and who has been severely hurt.

No matter how far one has strayed, the cross is home and home is near. And when one moves back home to the cross, everything is new. For the cross is all about resurrection and new birth. The past is gone and in fact, conquered. And though as for me, I cannot go back and become who I know God wanted me to be, I can be what he wants me to be now.

And I know he can use me in the place I'm in because I'm living at the foot of his son's cross. He is taking me as I am, and even at this older age, he is refining me to be a vessel of honor for his glory. I wasted his time and mine, but his mercy has given me a renewal. And now I'm his for his use.

It's unlikely I'll ever be in full-time ministry again as was intended. But full-time is relative. I may not be full-time by ministry standards, but I am full-time in the truest sense and more than I've ever been in my life. I'm living 24/7 at the cross.

Honestly, the devil tries to discourage me by reminding me of what could have been, but he is finding it harder and harder to do so as the cross becomes brighter in my path. The cross brightens, and Satan fades. As I study the word and listen to the voice from the cross, I can hardly hear Satan's words of defeat. His sifting days have ended.

I'm confident Satan will continue to try to keep me off path. But I'm not worried. I can't see him coming; I see the cross. I can't hear him speaking; I only hear words from the cross. I can feel his tempting power, but I feel a greater overcoming power oozing like a healing balm from the cross.

Satan cannot enter the perimeter of the cross. There is no room in between me and my savior. I'm working daily to keep it that way. My determination is fueled by the overcoming power of Jesus Christ. I will not be distracted again!

Epilogue

I was awake early on Sunday morning, as usual. I started the coffee and waited while the aroma filled the kitchen. The anticipation seemed to slow the brewing process. Knowing what the first morning sip was like, I was anxious to experience the euphoria that I knew was coming. Finally, *ahh,* no other taste like fresh brewed coffee.

With cup in hand, I stepped out onto my back patio. I looked up at the sky and admired its splendor. A small bird landed on the wooden fence about ten feet away and began chirping as if to say good morning. The dew glistened on my freshly cut grass. The wind was gently blowing through the leaves, and I thought to myself, this is a perfect day. And it would get even better as in just a few short hours, I would be doing what I love most. Standing in front of a small Sunday school class teaching the scriptures.

I went back inside and entered my study to read some scriptures. I read through tears the scriptures that had brought understanding and healing to my heart years before. In Luke chapter nine verse fifty-nine, Jesus is speaking.

> And he said unto another, "Follow me." But he said, "Lord, suffer me first to go and bury my father."
>
> Jesus said unto him, "Let the dead bury their dead: but go thou and preach the kingdom of God."

> And another also said, "Lord, I will follow thee; but let me first go bid them farewell, which are at home at my house."
>
> And Jesus said unto him, "No man, having put his hand to the plough, and looking back, is fit for the kingdom of God."

For so many years, I thought my dad had put the church before his sons. And I was bitter and jealous. I thought he had failed us. The truth is he did put the church before us. He answered the call, and nothing or no one would come ahead of that call to the ministry. My dad had heard Jesus calling him to follow. My dad answered, yes. My mom joined. They are the only two people I have ever met who answered the call as described by Jesus himself.

Now I know, I am not the only one who has sacrificed. My parents have had to rely on each other when friends were scarce. I've heard my mom say many times, "I don't have any friends." And I thought it was their fault. But it was the call. The call is a cross. Jesus said, "Take up thy cross and follow me." And they have.

There was no instruction book for Mom and Dad to read on how to raise preachers' kids. They simply did the best they could never wavering or compromising the call. Did they make mistakes? Yes. But they loved us and made sure we knew Jesus. What greater gift can a parent give than that of eternal life. Did their cross become ours to bear as well? Yes.

In the end, God has honored my parents for their faithfulness and determination through the lives of their sons and their children. All are following the Lord to the best of their ability. I would say that's a perfect track record.

With conscious intent, I have not written concerning the lives of my two brothers. I do not presume to speak for them. But this I know. Like all the preachers' kids before us, they have travelled on parallel roads. While the scenarios are different, they have been scarred and hurt just as deeply as I have. There has been no discussion with them on the content of this book and very little conversation concerning our adolescence. Therefore, my prayer for them is they find the same healing I have found and a newfound appreciation for the call to which Dad and Mom have been so faithful.

As for me, I am a new creature. No longer carrying the heavy baggage of dissolution, jealously, or bitterness. I don't feel the need to perform for anyone. The only one I answer to now is Jesus. My desire is to please him, and if I do that, what others think or believe is irrelevant.

No, I'm not where I thought I would be doing the thing I thought I would be doing at this time of my life, but I'm exactly where the Lord wants me to be for such a time as this. The evangelist was right, and Satan has sifted me like wheat. But he didn't win. I have complete peace and total victory in my savior. I don't know what lies ahead for me, but the past does not shape my future. God has that final say.

I can lift my hands toward him in humble praise and sing my favorite verse of "Amazing Grace." "Through many dangers, toils, and snares, I have already come. T'was grace that brought me safe this far and grace will lead me on."

What I thought was a curse for most of my life, I now embrace as my greatest blessing. My battle scars are now badges of honor. So it is with great humility and a deep sense of gratitude, I can boldly say without fear of implication, "My name is Frank Gray, and I am… the *son of a preacher!*"

To all who have shared my story and are not living at the cross, come home! You're always welcome here, and a brand-new start awaits you. Especially to the group for which I have written this book, preachers' kids. We share a special bond that no one else understands but him.

To all preachers' kids everywhere, meet me in heaven! Don't let anyone keep you from our reunion. It's going to be great over there!

About the Author

Frank Gray lives in Savannah, Georgia, and works in management for a large utility company. He serves in his dad's church as praise and worship leader and teaches an adult Sunday school class in addition to a weekly home study Bible class. He holds an associate in arts in general studies from Armstrong State College and a bachelor of science in business management from the University of Phoenix. He is divorced and the father of one daughter. He is a brass musician and has played in several bands and orchestras. His primary instrument is the trombone. Frank has been writing his book about his life as a preacher's son intermittently over four decades. His purpose for writing is to help other preacher's kids who have left the Gospel find their way back home. He also enjoys writing dramatic plays and has written over fifteen plays and produced eight. In his younger years, he served in full-time ministry as a youth pastor.

CPSIA information can be obtained
at www.ICGtesting.com
Printed in the USA
BVHW081549240220
573160BV00004B/661